WORK
COMES
THIRD

PRAISE FOR *WORK COMES THIRD*

"Danielle's book is a masterclass in tackling burnout, driven by her unrelenting passion to eradicate it. Her willingness to go above and beyond in understanding the issue shines through every page, as she combines deep learning with razor-sharp analytical skills to deliver the most detailed 'x-ray' of this modern epidemic. Whether you're stuck in the overwhelming grind of today's work culture or simply looking for a guide to reclaim your balance, this book is an absolute must-read. Insightful, empowering, practical, just like Danielle's coaching practice!"

— Senka Holzer, PhD
Author of *Be You: The Science of Becoming the Self You Were Born to Be*

"*Work Comes Third* is a refreshing, much-needed guide for leaders who care about their people. Packed with relatable stories and practical ideas, it shows how to create workplaces where everyone can thrive without burning out. Danielle offers a fresh perspective on eradicating burn-out, emphasizing that true success begins when we prioritize wellbeing. I've seen firsthand how this approach transforms overwhelmed leaders and weary employees into resilient, engaged individuals. This book is a must-read for anyone who wants to lead with heart and build a thriving team."

— Natalie Siston
Professional Speaker, Coach, and Bestselling Author of
Let Her Out: Reclaim Who You Have Always Been

"If you've experienced the exhaustion of burnout, then *Work Comes Third* is for you. With great honesty and vulnerability, Danielle Collins shares her own dark descent to burnout. Her inspiring stories and perseverance, as well as her science-based strategies, provide a clear path back to wellbeing."

— Jim Strohecker
Co-creator, Wellness Inventory Certification Training

"With refreshing openness, insight, and humor, Danielle Collins reveals a roadmap to journey from the depths of burnout to renewed purpose, energy, and fulfillment. A must-read for all leaders and anyone ready to thrive both personally and professionally!"

— Adam David Russ
Teacher and award-winning author of *Bloodhound in Blue*

"Danielle Collins' *Work Comes Third* is a lifeline for anyone facing burnout and a must-read for anyone striving to create a more balanced life. This book is packed with practical, down-to-earth solutions that go beyond surface-level advice, empowering readers to cultivate wellbeing both at work and in their personal lives.

"What truly sets this book apart is Danielle's authenticity. Her candid stories about her own experiences with burnout and her transformative journey to recovery are deeply relatable and inspiring. Her insights serve as a reminder that it's possible to not only bounce back, but also build a life filled with purpose and joy.

"This book is a fabulous resource for anyone looking to reclaim their energy, passion, and sense of self. Highly recommended!"

— Cathy Fyock, author of *Writer Crisis Hotline*

"When I reflect on my decades as a superintendent of schools, I was always searching for ways to motivate my staff and help them be their best. *Work Comes Third* provides a blueprint for not only retaining your staff, but also for taking better care of yourself (and I wish I'd had access to its wisdom at the beginning of my career). The author's journey is an eye-opener, not to be ignored!"

— Dorothea M. Shannon, EdD
Retired School Superintendent

"This book is a must-read for anyone, boss or employee, who has ever felt burned out or exploited by their employer. Ms. Collins' focus on the 10 Dimensions of Wellbeing is urgently needed in our fast-paced and profit-based world. I highly recommend *Work Comes Third* for individuals feeling stuck in difficult jobs, as the author offers hope and solutions for these overworked employees."

— Celia Bavier
Executive Director, Border Community Alliance (BCA)

"Required reading for anyone entering the job force. Collins' honesty reflects a cautionary tale that pivots to one of hope and optimism. And reminds us that our inner critic could lead us to self-destruct."

— Tim S., Former Burnout Sufferer and Client

"This book unlocks strategies for avoiding or overcoming burnout for team leaders and employees alike. I have found Collins' advice approachable and easily applicable. A must-read for anyone looking for a reset in their work-life balance!"

— Bethy Hardeman, Fintech Marketer and Team Leader

"Danielle coached me for years and I grew in countless ways while working with her. This book distills her wisdom into powerful insights you can use right now."

— Ezra Fox, Founder, Chaotic Good Studios

"Danielle delivers the very message we need when we've lost our personal identities to corporate personas made for resumes and LinkedIn. This book helps the reader acknowledge the toxic societal pressures of work before everything else and serves as a practical guide for finding true wellbeing."

— Allison Scoggin, CFP®

"*Work Comes Third* is a wise and pragmatic approach to wellness. Danielle Collins' story about being overworked is all too familiar in today's toxic work culture, but her self-reflection about burning out is refreshingly honest. She says out loud what most of us keep quietly inside. If you want to retain your most valuable employees and see them thrive, carefully ponder her tips for team leaders. Don't just read this book—put her advice into practice. You'll be so glad that you did!"

— Julie Abouzelof, Small Business Owner

"*Work Comes Third* wonderfully lays out how to live a more healthy and purposeful life. Danielle elaborates from her own experiences with burnout and expertly draws a roadmap that shows us how to live from our values and increase our wellbeing. Having lived through burnout myself in the workplace, I wish that this book had been available to me many years ago. It is an absolute must-read for any leader or employee striving for sustainability and improved work performance."

— Paul Carlson, MBA, Life Coach and Administrative Director

"*Work Comes Third* is the book you are looking for, whether you are new to the experience of burnout or you've been fighting it for years. It is filled with an abundance of simple but highly effective ways to restore your wellbeing and positively impact all aspects of your life. I turned the last page of this book with a sense of optimism and hope. I'm inspired to make a lasting change in my life, and it will do the same for you!"

— Erin Bialecki, Nonprofit Fundraising Leader

"Burned out with your job? Engage in this insightful conversation with Danielle as she guides you through the steps toward a well-balanced life. Embrace your authenticity, pursue your passions, and say 'NO' without guilt. This book will help you thrive and is a game-changer for our society. Together, 'We Can Do This!'"

— Mary Earle Stallings, Retired Teacher and Librarian

"This is more than Danielle's burnout survival story—it's a call to discover yourself, recognize your inherent worth, and unleash your unique gifts through your vocation. This book packs lived experience, theory, and exercises that combine for an actionable path to personal and professional fulfillment. It's the antidote to an outdated belief system that success demands sacrificing one's mind, body, and spirit. I'd call it 'required reading for strivers.'"

— Liza Horan, Host of *Express Yourself with Authenticity* Podcast

WORK COMES THIRD

Eradicating Burnout in
Overwhelmed Leaders and
Their Weary Employees

E. DANIELLE COLLINS

Publishing support provided by
Ignite Press
55 Shaw Ave. Suite 204
Clovis, CA 93612
www.IgnitePress.us

ISBN: 979-8-9927702-0-9
ISBN: 979-8-9927702-1-6 (E-book)

For bulk purchases and for booking, contact:

Danielle Collins
Danielle@PrimaveraStrategies.com
PrimaveraStrategies.com

Library of Congress Control Number: 2025903471

Cover design by Jeerald Bokilis
Edited by Cathy Cruise
Interior design by Jetlaunch
Cover photography by Danielle Collins
Author photo by Bobak Radbin

FIRST EDITION

To Molly, Boo, and Scout (my beloved border collies)—
thank you for teaching me that you come before work.

TABLE OF CONTENTS

LETTER TO MY READER

My Friend,

You have arrived feeling overwhelmed and weary, a faded version of yourself that you no longer recognize. You may be wondering if you should linger. You may be wondering if you belong.

Welcome. Linger. You are not alone, and you belong.

As we sink under the weight of our unsustainable workloads, we blame ourselves, and then discover our spirits are desiccated and our bodies are ailing. Burnout is a societal issue, not a personal problem, and we are neck-deep in this workplace emergency.

I wrote this book for you as a rallying cry for radical transformation of our working world. Join me in pioneering a movement where *Work Comes Third*. Together, we'll create a "Culture of Wellbeing," where all employees are cherished, allowing leaders to retain their valuable staff and fulfill their missions.

There are some things I want you to know as you begin reading *Work Comes Third*. I am a previous fundraiser and burnout survivor myself, and I know well the isolation and despair you may be feeling. I turned my burnout into a vocation to help others cope with the crisis, and today I'm a coach, author, and speaker.

Work Comes Third is a guide for overwhelmed leaders and their weary employees to prevail over burnout. I offer insights for team leaders as well as team members throughout the book.

I did NOT use artificial intelligence in writing my manuscript, beyond the spell check in Microsoft Word. This is my own creative effort. In addition, artists did not use AI in the creation of the cover.

I have changed the names of many people in the book.

I use the word "wellbeing" to describe our welfare on all levels—physical, emotional, mental, and spiritual. In our society, the word "wellness" often refers to the health of our bodies alone. I use the phrase "mental fitness" to describe an exciting mindset that everyone can enjoy, while "mental health" reminds us of disorders and psychiatric care.

The suggestions I share are evidence-based. I experienced burnout firsthand and can attest to the symptoms and survival stories. In addition, I base my tips on research by scientists, and you can find these sources at the end of the book.

Finally, I end each chapter with a rousing, "*We can do it!*" This harkens back to my love and respect for Rosie the Riveter. She represents the women in the 1940s who shattered glass ceilings while building ships, planes, tanks, and weapons. Their round-the-clock efforts made the United States a military and economic world power by the end of World War II, and their defense of democracy resonates today.

If you're ready to find your dedication and passion again, then keep reading. If you're ready to dispel the painful myth that you're weak if you're burning out, then keep reading. If you want to transform your own life, as well as your organization—then turn the page, my friend, and keep reading. You have in your hands the key to great change.

We can do it!

1

DESCENDING TO BURNOUT

After dragging myself to work, bleary-eyed and apprehensive, I arrived in time for the "team" meeting. As I settled into the heavy chair at the conference table, I noticed the furrowed brows of my fellow fundraisers and sensed their palpable disapproval. Yesterday, I had arrived at the office an hour late, and today we would discuss the impact of my irresponsible behavior.

My boss, Michelle, finished talking about the upcoming board meeting, and pushed her short, blonde hair behind her ear. She averted her eyes, and I uneasily watched her profile.

"Let's switch gears. From now on, there will be no personal appointments between the hours of 8:00 a.m. and 5:00 p.m.," she decreed.

My stomach lurched and my hands felt clammy as I fiddled with my pen. *Can she do that?* I wondered. *We're salaried, hard-working employees. Why is she treating me like a kid who can't be trusted?*

Michelle continued to avoid my eyes and refused to address me directly. I was stunned that she was suggesting that we ignore our most basic needs. No annual exams, skin cancer screenings, or pap smears. No visits to the physical therapist, dentist, or podiatrist. No therapy sessions, vet visits, or emergency appointments with the plumber. *WTF?*

My brain still boggles over this. Were we supposed to give up doctors we trust for ones that can see us at 7:00 in the morning? What if the dog walkers can't take care of my sweet border collie? What if we have school-age kids? What if our friend needs help after surgery? What if we're taking care of an ailing parent? Life happens during work hours too, regardless of the rules we construct around it.

I considered talking to HR about the decree but unfortunately decided not to, as the shame crept in. The voices in my head were persistent and unforgiving:

I was noticeably late for work.
My actions were the seeds of this terrible managerial decision.
I knew for months that I was struggling and now everyone else knew it too.
I was weak for being in this constant state of exhaustion.

This felt especially painful to me, because my boss and I previously had a foundation of trust. I felt like she'd forgotten who I fundamentally was—a passionate, creative, and dedicated worker.

What naughtiness had led to my tardiness that fateful morning—and was it worth the price I paid?

While it is true that I have shown up for work with a post-orgasmic glow, sex was not the reason I was late. Nor did I oversleep. I did have an appointment with my mechanic at BC Automotive to change the oil on my little Corolla.

I loved BC Automotive more than many of my boyfriends. They took excellent care of my car and were trustworthy, time and again. They never talked down to me as a woman and they kept my Corolla sparkling inside and out. I had happily given them my business for over a decade.

BC Automotive was not open on the weekends (good for them!) and they regularly serviced my car first thing in the morning on a weekday. The day before, they had told me (with apologies) that they were missing a part they needed for my oil change, and it would take an additional 20 to 30 minutes. I realized I'd be late for work, but this was unavoidable. I was salaried and had no pressing meetings that morning.

I needed my car to do my job and visit major donors, and my car needed an oil change. I wasn't married and I took care of the car, house, and dog myself. In hindsight, I can see that my own wellbeing was even further down on the list.

When I arrived at the office, I was met by my coworker, who wanted to know where I'd been. I confirmed that I'd been to BC Automotive, like I'd shared in my public calendar.

My coworker then asked, "Are you late because you were soliciting them for a corporate gift?"

"No," I replied, desperately trying not to roll my eyes. "I didn't solicit them. I got my oil changed." End of story.

But it wasn't the end, because shortly thereafter, another coworker barged into my office.

"My husband and I specifically chose our auto mechanic based on their Saturday availability," she gloated.

Wow. I looked down at my thumbs and considered jamming them into my eyeballs. *What business is it of hers how I chose my mechanic? I feel SO misunderstood.* I didn't bother explaining how I based my decision on trust and longevity. In fact, I applauded that they took care of their employees and gave them weekends to recuperate. In hindsight, I wish my coworker and I could have had a real conversation.

She stalked out of my office, and I hoped that was the end of it. Of course, it wasn't. While my boss didn't say anything at the time, she saved her malice for our staff meeting.

For the first time, we were behind in our fundraising goals, and Michelle was resorting to ridiculous, fear-based tactics. Every day, she demanded that we meet our ambitious goal—and every day, I remembered that this goal was arbitrary and not based on fundraising history. She made it up (as best she could) to mollify her own demanding boss, the executive director.

Michelle also had promised us we'd hire a team of 10 people to accomplish the wildly ambitious goals of her three-year plan. When her boss eventually refused to let her hire the full team of people, Michelle didn't decrease our fundraising goals respectively. I had enough development experience to understand this was a serious misstep. How many people were on our team at the time of the hiring freeze? Four. Four people struggling to do the work of 10.

I believe that Michelle's fears about "underachievement" drove her to create a hard-hearted, if not toxic culture where her employees would never again dare to take care of their cars and roll in an hour late. In her mind, we didn't deserve it until we had reached the financial goal.

I found her demands intolerable, and I refused to stop attending to my basic needs. I did, however, stop sharing on our public calendar any incriminating personal information.

Ideally, my boss and I would have talked about my unsustainable workload that left me feeling fatigued and overwhelmed. We would have discussed my challenges of juggling my tasks at home with my responsibilities at work. Also, my boss would have nipped in the bud the meddling and overreach of pesky coworkers. More than anything, I wanted compassion and flexibility in the workplace—not rejection and rigidity. I had been feeling for a while that I didn't fit in, and this incident with BC Automotive convinced me I was right. This was a turning point for me in that job, and I never again felt like part of the team.

Feeling exhausted, cynical, and disconnected, I viewed the oil change as a major wake-up call that it was time for me to begin a new adventure. I'm grateful to this day that Michelle so clearly showed us how little she cared about our wellbeing with her tiresome and impossible demands that work must come first.

Work Comes Third

When I burned out, I faced an impossible choice. I could take care of myself with healthy boundaries between work and home, or, as a fundraiser for nonprofits, I could work longer hours day after day. I knew how much funding was needed to fulfill our mission, and ultimately reduce the suffering of others. In addition, fundraisers often are painfully aware that these precious dollars prevent job layoffs, including their own.

Hardworking folks in many professions face similar choices that feel impossible. Even before the pandemic, teachers were overwhelmed and underfunded. Health-care workers are still reeling from treating millions of patients with the coronavirus. Social workers experience compassion fatigue as they help traumatized clients deal with abuse and violence. Tech workers endure poor leadership and toxic work cultures, while attorneys suffer from all work and no play. Retail workers, sales personnel, emergency responders, and government employees are all burning out.

Our approach to work isn't working. How are we to choose ourselves in a culture that celebrates overwork as a badge of honor?

On my road to burning out, I wholeheartedly believed that work comes first, and I didn't choose to take care of my own needs. While I ignored my physical, emotional, and spiritual requirements, I developed a hiatal hernia from the stress; I felt ashamed for feeling exhausted; and I was out of touch with my rich spiritual life that usually sustains me. I abandoned myself.

> We're accustomed to the tenet that work comes first, and this destructive idea is so ingrained that we rarely question its validity.

We're accustomed to the tenet that work comes first, and this destructive idea is so ingrained that we rarely question its validity. In fact, when I tried typing "Work Comes Third" in my word document, my fingers unconsciously typed "Work Comes First," not once, but multiple times.

What does it mean if our *Work Comes Third*? It means that our job isn't our top priority (OMG), and it also means that our job isn't even our second priority (WTF). In our work-obsessed culture, it's hard to remember what needs to come first, so to be at your tippy-top best, these must be your priorities:

1. Your own wellbeing
2. The wellbeing of your family, however you define it (my family includes my dog!)
3. Work

This list of priorities may seem radical, but it's what will save you from the misery of burnout. When we give ourselves permission to take care of our own health and wellbeing, and our family's, we reduce our stress and increase our resilience.

How could I have given myself permission to take better care of ME? I needed to put myself first, but I had no models at work who prioritized their own self-care. In hindsight, I have compassion for the person I was then, and I see now that the idea of putting my own needs first is countercultural.

Prioritizing my family to be second—after my own needs, yet before work—is downright revolutionary. It seems obvious to say this, but let me spell it out. If we don't take care of ourselves first, then we have nothing left to give when it's time to take Scout to the vet. As the flight attendants instruct, we must put on our own oxygen masks first before we can help others. Likewise, taking care of our family supersedes work because, ultimately, our inner circle is a bigger priority. (And if it's not, it should be!) We'll be more focused and creative at work when our family is healthy and fulfilled. In fact, when we take care of ourselves first and our family second, we'll be better employees.

Did you see how I just said that we can justify putting ourselves first, and work third, because ultimately we'll be better employees? **This is still putting work first!** I wrote that sentence because I wanted to point out that we justify taking care of ourselves if we can then show we'll be more creative and productive at work. We're itchy and uncomfortable with the idea that we innately deserve greater wellbeing. We reject this notion because it's ingrained in us that we must relentlessly prove our value, and we believe the dangerous myth that external measures of our success demonstrate our worth. Yet these measures create troubling detours from ultimately building a life of meaning and connection.

My friend, you and I were born inherently worthy. Self-care is not a prize for struggling at work; it is our birthright. YES!

It turns out that two things can be true at the same time: (1) our wellbeing is more important than our accomplishments at work, and (2) when we take care of ourselves first and our family second, we will be better employees. In this book, I will share many ideas to build a Culture of Wellbeing, and I recognize the importance of persuading unsure leaders that it will give your organization a strategic advantage. So while many of the suggestions will help you become a better employee, my hope for you is that you appreciate your awesome self and remember your intrinsic value.

My Descent to Burnout

Looking back, it's not a surprise that, after a long career as a fundraiser, I burned out. Quite spectacularly. I understand now that it's our duty as individuals, as well as the responsibility of organizations, to make sure that our *Work Comes Third*.

You might wonder if I lacked passion for the goals of the organizations. That's an interesting idea, but don't misunderstand—I was passionate about the mission of every nonprofit where I worked. My passion, however, had transformed into exhaustion and my body, mind, and spirit were depleted.

You might wonder if I'm inherently lazy. Great question, but "super-duper motivated" is a better description of how I'm wired. I was distressed by my personal journey as I moved from being a dedicated, hardworking employee to someone who lacked joy and enthusiasm. I felt spent at all levels and was unable to renew my internal resources.

She must be strangely flawed and weak, you say. Yep, this is another reasonable thought (and I wondered this myself)—but the truth is, I'm a human being who can complete many tasks thrown at her, but not forever. Yes, in hindsight I see there were ways I could have taken better care of myself, but what is also true is that if I was burning out, there were leadership issues, creating an environment that celebrated overwork.

Burning out for me became a major life event that I wouldn't wish on anyone. I quit my job and was shocked how long it took me to heal (years). I'm happy to share that I realized how important it was for me to build a career that was better aligned with my values. I went back to school, and today I'm a coach, author, and speaker, helping people who are burning out to renew their passion. I love my job, and I'm eager to help you prevail over burnout.

My Top Questions

My burnout happened one day at a time, over the course of a few years. During this period of my life, I asked myself many questions, over and over. As I recovered, I tried to find answers to better understand what the hell happened, and I've spent years learning about the impacts of overwork and fatigue, as well as the opposite—wellbeing. I'm a learner at heart and will likely always continue to seek answers. This book is my way of sharing everything I've learned, so that not only can you avoid making the same mistakes, but you'll also reclaim lost energy from the vortex of burnout. Now, more than ever, the world needs you to be a force for good. Below are the questions I noodled over.

I'm responsible for my own actions, so what was my role in my burnout?

After my first successful capital campaign, I understood the energy required for these multiyear, transformational efforts. These campaigns

are as exciting as they are exhaust-
ing, and they help an organization do
amazing things (like expand hospital
facilities, establish scholarships, or protect land in perpetuity). I agreed to do
a second campaign, and then a third,
even though I was increasingly fatigued.
Why? Because I had a voice in my head
that told me my value was based on
what I achieved, and that's not true. My
value is based on who I am intrinsically, and so is yours—and it takes courage to recognize our inherent worth in
a society bent on overwork. We'll look
at our mean-spirited voices in-depth
in Chapter 8 – Boosting Your Mental
Fitness, so stay tuned.

*I had a massage and took a hot bath, but I
still feel stressed. Why?*

Self-care isn't
about pedicures,
but it *is* about
self-preservation,
survival, and taking
responsibility for
our basic needs. It's
a holistic approach
that addresses your
body, mind, and
spirit and helps
you enjoy ultimate
wellbeing.

The more exhausted I became, the less these indulgences made a
difference. These treats are enjoyable in the moment, but they're a tiny
bandage on the bigger problem of overwork and burnout. Self-care isn't
about pedicures, but it *is* about self-preservation, survival, and taking
responsibility for our basic needs. It's a holistic approach that addresses
your body, mind, and spirit and helps you enjoy ultimate wellbeing.

*Why, when I was unhappy at work, did it affect all the other dimensions
of my life?*

In my coach training, I was excited to learn that all the different areas of our lives are connected, and what we do in one impacts the others.

We can use this knowledge to our benefit, and we'll talk about this in detail in Chapter 3 – Discovering the 10 Dimensions of Wellbeing.

Was I fundamentally weak?

No. That's an ugly lie society tells us. And you're not weak either, so don't let anyone tell you otherwise.

Is there something wrong with me for not wanting to be a "workhorse?"

Shortly before I left the fundraising industry, I entertained the idea of other development jobs, one of which was at a university where they were "looking for workhorses." I was exhausted and didn't want to be a workhorse ever again, and I recognized I was not a consumable to be discarded. I wanted to be valued, appreciated, and respected. I wanted a happy life at work and beyond, not one where I was too tired to pursue my own creative projects. Looking back, I'm glad I listened to my inner voice that warned against accepting another job where I'd play the role of workhorse. There's nothing wrong with me for wanting more, and likewise, there's nothing wrong with you.

I earn $X. If I'm getting paid to be the best, don't I owe my organization all the necessary overtime?

Many people believe this to be true. In fact, I believed it myself, for years. If I'm getting paid a certain amount, doesn't this mean the organization owns my time outside of work? Don't I have to be available 24/7? This belief leads to concerns that a much-needed raise, while desirable, will actually lead to selling our souls—so let's stay underpaid and unappreciated.

We have bought into a debilitating myth. While higher pay is likely equated with more responsibility, the leaders with more responsibility are humans. They have the same need to rejuvenate as everyone else and they inherently deserve this. In addition, healthy organizations want peak performance from their employees, and they understand that for everyone to be at their best, all employees need a full life outside of work.

When each of us can take care of ourselves and our families, we're free to create greatness at work. Also, it is the leaders who model wellbeing for their employees who inspire loyalty and dedication.

When exactly did I burn out?

I've realized I didn't suddenly burn out. It was a slow journey on a continuum, with health and wellbeing on one end, and overwhelm and fatigue at the other. I am certified in multiple coach-training programs, and at the Wellness Inventory Certification Training, I learned the importance of examining every day which way we're facing on the continuum. Are we taking small steps toward wellbeing? Or are we facing in the opposite direction, striding toward premature death?

How might I have prevented myself from burning out?

In hindsight, I see that I had drained my energy reserves. Since then, I've learned there are ways we can boost our resilience, such as establishing healthy boundaries between work and home, being genuine at work, and enjoying a mindset of gratitude. We'll discuss these in detail.

What were the leadership issues that led to my burnout?

Overwork was a key issue. One supervisor demanded that we have staff meetings at 6:30 in the morning, so that we could meet with our donors between 8:00 a.m. and 5:00 p.m., and then attend occasional evening events. For me, a night-owl, this was a brutal morning schedule and therefore a shortcut to exhaustion. I do my best work later in the day, and no office policy will change the way I'm wired. This leads me to another leadership issue that I've encountered—an expectation that staff fit the mold of an **"ideal employee"** who is always available. No one is always available. No one. There's no room for authenticity in this environment, and to be "professional," we leave big, important pieces of ourselves at home. The result—we feel like round pegs in square holes and experience cynicism toward our colleagues. A third leadership issue I faced was a mismatch of **values**. I felt confused and lost when my manager stopped being curious about what motivated me, and instead demanded I raise money, not to fulfill our mission, but to assuage the ego of her boss. We'll discuss the importance of understanding our core values in Chapter 12 – Fulfilling Your Purpose.

The Pivotal Question that Launched My Career

After enthusiastically quitting my job as a fundraiser, I returned to school, this time to become a professional coach. I couldn't wait to help people who were burning out. I felt good about completing a rigorous, coach-training program at the local university, and I was reaching out to fellow fundraisers to learn more about their needs at work.

I spent time with Francie, a former colleague I met with after becoming a coach, and she had politely listened to how I hoped to help. We were standing in a stairway as I prepared to leave, when Francie shared, **"What we really want, Danielle, is to retain our valuable employees. How can you help us with that?"**

What a fantastic question! And my stomach knotted as I realized that, despite my training, I didn't have the answer. (Yet!) I knew how to coach effectively and apply core competencies. I knew my own devastating experience of burnout. But I didn't have a plan for how Francie could retain her staff. I also didn't know what to offer to help Francie put her own basic needs first.

I redoubled my efforts to answer Francie's question. I instinctively understood that the opposite of burnout was total wellbeing—of our minds, bodies, and spirits. Studying wellbeing became a way for me to create effective coaching programs and transform the lives of my clients. In the past, I knew how to recognize the symptoms of burnout, and now my expanded focus on wellbeing allowed me to help my clients boost their resilience, enjoy greater fulfillment and purpose, and experience peak performance.

As I became an expert on wellbeing, I recognized that I had remained in "Burnout Central" as a fundraiser longer than necessary. There were specific and meaningful actions I could have taken to preserve my health, but I had abandoned my own needs, hour after hour, day after day.

Sleep? Certainly sleep was not as important as showing up on time, even after a late night at work. Healthy food? Who knew what was healthy when I was eating in my car? Cherishing my body? I had a faint memory of yoga and meditation. Mental fitness? My inner critic was telling me I was ineffective and weak, thank you very much, and that was a good thing, because without this unkind voice I'd surely be a slovenly, lazy, unkempt employee.

Through my intense studies of wellbeing and burnout, I learned there are many, many ways that we can improve our self-care. I developed an innovative framework that I now champion, that focuses on the 10 Dimensions of Wellbeing that will decrease our burnout.

While there are lots of things we can do to help ourselves as individuals, if I'm burning out, then there are leadership issues as well. Organizations benefit from a Culture of Wellbeing because burnout is not an individual problem. In fact, creating this Culture of Wellbeing is the answer to how we can retain our valuable employees. Let's create a new working world where employees are cherished!

If my own story resonates, you'll want to keep reading. You are not alone, and there is hope! Also, as we move forward together, consider if any of your staff might be struggling. Coming up next, we'll discuss the key symptoms of burnout.

We can do it!

2

TALLYING THE COSTS OF BURNOUT

I hunched over the steering wheel of my parked car, clutching my cell phone. I wiped away tears, took a deep breath, and called my longtime friend from high school. After the BC Automotive incident, I made my way through my days at work by exiting the office when I felt overwhelmed and calling friends or family for support. They all had different ways of saying the same thing (your boss considers you expendable), but I wasn't ready to quit. I was managing a capital campaign, and I wanted to successfully complete it before I resigned.

As I waited for my friend to answer, my brain rolled quickly through all my work responsibilities. Not only was I strategizing for a capital campaign, but I was also thanking donors by sharing stories of our success, meeting with people who might want to support our efforts, speaking publicly, participating in countless board and team meetings, writing grants and direct mail, organizing events, and generating staff support. Plus, we were expected to meet our goals understaffed. *Holy crap.* No wonder I was exhausted well before I arrived home.

My BFF didn't answer, and my eyes filled with tears again. *Ugh.* I was grateful for everyone's support, but I had noticed that not one person said, "I understand. I've experienced that too." No one really knew what to do with me and I couldn't help but wonder if they thought there was something inherently wrong with me for finally splintering under the weight of my responsibilities.

I hope that when you read this book, not only will you feel seen and accepted, but you'll also learn concrete steps you can take to reverse your journey back to wellbeing. First, let's consider the great toll of burnout, on ourselves as individuals, as it impacts all areas of our lives. There are also inordinate costs for organizations that struggle with burnout and the high turnover rates that follow.

Burnout is a global problem, and it's getting worse. Many thanks to the World Health Organization (WHO), which in 2019 described the three key symptoms employees experience when they're burning out: (1) exhaustion, (2) cynicism, and (3) ineffectiveness. The WHO describes burnout as an "occupational phenomenon" due to stress in the workplace. I think this is a limited perspective. After a pandemic where single parents made impossible choices between helping their kids with online school, completing their own work responsibilities, and also taking care of their own parents who were struggling with COVID, it's clear we can burn out from crises at home too.

1. **Exhaustion**

   When we're exhausted, we feel overextended and fatigued. It's a sure sign of work overload, which is a management issue. I've heard some declare that we experience exhaustion only within our physical bodies. My exhaustion, however, was all-inclusive. I was physically, emotionally, mentally, and spiritually depleted, and it took me years to heal.

2. **Cynicism**

   We may have cold attitudes toward our colleagues. As our passion is replaced by cynicism, we might believe we don't share anything in common with the people we work with. We feel jaded about a job we once loved.

3. **Ineffectiveness**

People who are burning out may feel inadequate. We feel less and less effective with each project. When we forget our past accomplishments, our self-esteem suffers, and our colleagues question our abilities.

Have you experienced any of these symptoms? You also may be wondering about your employees, so keep in mind that the image people project to the outside world does not always match their internal state. (This was true for me.) People may seem calm, trying to appear "professional," when in fact they're upset. It's critical that you build trust, so they can share what's really going on under the surface.

As I began my new coaching business, I interviewed dozens of people who were overwhelmed at work to better understand their experiences. I looked for common themes to use in my articles on burnout. Below, I've grouped some of their comments by burnout symptom.

What does "exhaustion" sound like? I heard people say:

I have no more to give.
My stomach is always in knots (and a host of other physical issues, including poor sleep and diseases).
I'm an adrenaline junkie, jumping from fire to fire.
Work issues take up all the space in my mind.
I experience brain fog; my thinking is frazzled.
The job sucks away at my soul.
I'm not honoring myself.
This isn't the life I want to live.

What does "cynicism" sound like? People shared:

I'm feeling inauthentic.
They don't respect me as a person.

I don't fit in with these people.
Nothing we do is right.
I have a "screw you" attitude.
How do you deal with a boss who says, "I don't care, just get it done"?

What does feeling "ineffective" sound like? I heard folks share:

I'm in survival mode.
I'm constantly doubting myself.
Who will I disappoint?
It's impossible to put everyone first.
I feel panicky that I'll blow it.
No matter how hard I try, they'll never be happy.
I'm not good enough.

These are the words of people who were once passionate and committed to their organizations. Over time, they became deeply dissatisfied. Which statements most resonated with you?

When Our Psychological Needs Go Unmet

In the 1970s, two psychologists began collaborating at the University of Rochester and they reframed our assumptions about what motivates us as humans. Previously, we had focused on the idea of external motivation, with reward and punishment being key. Dr. Richard Ryan and Dr. Edward Deci, however, saw the limits of external motivation, and they created a new theory that has resonated ever since. They demonstrated that *intrinsic motivations* are more important. They offered the world their Self-Determination Theory and described three basic psychological needs. When we meet these needs, we feel fulfilled and we thrive. When our basic needs are unmet, we suffer. What are our three basic psychological needs?

1. **Autonomy**
   We thrive when we're in charge of our own life and choices, and we feel good when we can solve our own problems and take the initiative.

2. **Relatedness** (I prefer the term "Connection")
   We're biologically designed for connection, so we thrive in a healthy community. Understanding that we're a valued and integral member of the team feels good!

3. **Competence**
   We feel effective and confident in our ability to make a difference for our team and organization.

I began to wonder what happens at work when these three basic psychological needs go unmet. It occurred to me that each of these needs is directly related to the symptoms of burnout described by the World Health Organization. When our psychological needs are unfilled, we experience corresponding symptoms of burnout. You can see in the picture below how a lack of autonomy leads to exhaustion, because we're not empowered to say NO to an unsustainable workload. A lack of connection with your coworkers leads to cynicism and distrust of your team. And experiencing a lack of competence makes us believe we're ineffective and inadequate.

The Impact of Not Fulfilling Our Psychological Needs at Work

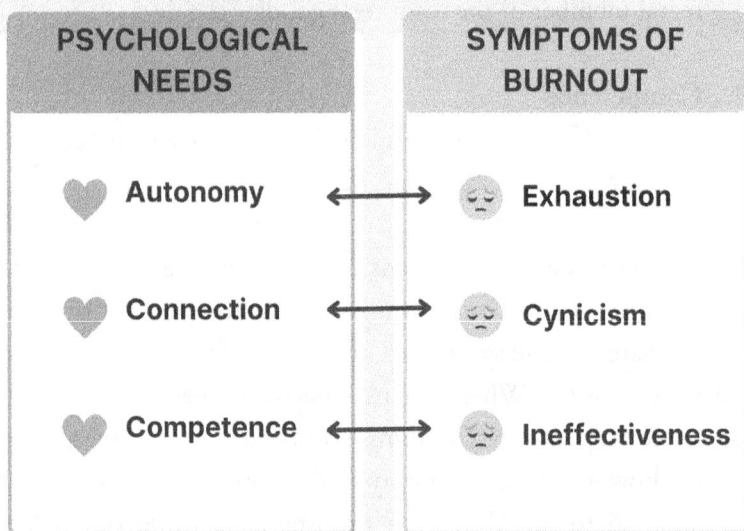

PSYCHOLOGICAL NEEDS	SYMPTOMS OF BURNOUT
♥ Autonomy ←→	😞 Exhaustion
♥ Connection ←→	😞 Cynicism
♥ Competence ←→	😞 Ineffectiveness

When our psychological needs go unmet, we experience corresponding symptoms of burnout.

Work Comes Third
by E. Danielle Collins

It's no wonder that the symptoms of burnout hurt so much! They are the painful outcome when we've starved our psychological needs. These symptoms poke us directly in our primal wounds, so please, have great compassion for yourself if you're suffering.

Folks who are new to the working world sometimes choose unfulfilling jobs, thinking that they can find their fulfillment outside of work. We need to thoughtfully pay attention to our most basic psychological needs and determine if they can be met at work. If they can't, over time it will likely lead to burnout. Also, when we tell ourselves we'll have the energy to pursue our creative passions outside of work, we need to be honest with ourselves. Will you have the energy after hours? Are you working at an organization that delights in your outside activities? Or are you working in an environment that merely tolerates it and expects you to be available on weekends? These are critical things to understand as you make your way through your career and life.

> Whatever you do, choose jobs that allow you to experience autonomy, connection, and competence. This is as important, if not more so, than your salary.

Whatever you do, choose jobs that allow you to experience autonomy, connection, and competence. This is as important, if not more so, than your salary.

Let's consider the organizational issues that impact the wellbeing of employees and lead to burnout.

Six Key Contributors to Burnout

1. **Workload**

   Ideally, our work is manageable, at a rate that's sustainable. Over the decades, our jobs have become much more emotionally intense and intellectually demanding, and in many professions, we no longer enjoy slower periods of work. Instead, we jump from one goal to the next, rarely stopping to commemorate our progress. It's time to recognize the stress is chronic, not short-term.

   Regrettably, in our culture we applaud overwork and constant busyness, thinking that our inherent value is derived from our latest achievement as we seek external validation. Overwhelm often begins when the responsibilities of previous employees are reassigned to the remaining staff.

2. **Reward**

   Remember that money is a top reason people leave. In the past, there was an unhealthy expectation that employees should undervalue themselves because they're passionate about the work of the organization, but this is an outdated way of thinking, and in reality, their passion doesn't pay their bills. Their ample paycheck does.

   While we need to be paid what we're worth, studies show that we also crave the intrinsic reward of enjoyable work, and we thrive when we understand how we helped our organization fulfill its mission.

3. **Fairness**

   We experience fairness when we feel respected by our bosses, boards, and colleagues. In addition, we lose trust when our organizations send the message that money is more important than employees.

4. **Autonomy**

   As we discussed, one of our basic psychological needs is autonomy. While we thrive when we're responsible for our own choices, we see micromanagement as a lack of trust. When we need more control over making our own decisions, we feel frustrated and trapped—a sure route to exhaustion.

   Many employees flourished while working from home during the pandemic, and they may now expect more control over their work.

5. **Values**

   When our core values aren't aligned with the values of our organization, we may burn out, and we'll talk about this in Chapter 12 — Fulfilling Your Purpose. We may also feel cynical when there is a difference between what the organization says it values versus what it actually does.

6. **Community**

   A healthy community meets our need for connection. In fact, having a good friend at work helps us feel more engaged. Ongoing conflict, however, is destructive and makes us less productive.

The six factors that lead to burnout originally appeared in the presentation, "The Science of Burnout," by Emiliana Simon-Thomas, Science Director at UC Berkeley's Greater Good Science Center.

Calculating the Organizational Costs of Burnout

When employees burn out, they're likely to leave, and the turnover rate in some organizations is a clarion call for change. A position vacancy may increase the workloads of the remaining employees, reduce team spirit, decrease performance, squander institutional knowledge, sever relationships with stakeholders, disrupt critical services, and increase the costs of recruitment.

Organizations that create a Culture of Wellbeing have a competitive edge. In a recent Deloitte study of over 3,000 people across four countries, the majority of employees, managers, and upper-echelon executives are thinking about quitting—for a job that improves their wellbeing. Furthermore, these organizations with a Culture of Wellbeing have a strategic advantage, as they will retain their valuable employees, reduce their costs, and fulfill their missions.

A Culture of Wellbeing is the remedy to an overworked world. Leaders understand that every employee, including leaders themselves, must put their own self-care first. They actively address the leadership issues (like overwork and micromanagement) that lead to burnout, and they focus on boosting resilience and building a foundation of trust.

For Chapters 2 to 13, I'm going to share **Tips for Team Leaders**. If you're not a team leader and instead are a team member, please read every tip and apply it to yourself so that you can boost your own resilience. In addition, by understanding what I'm suggesting for leaders, you can think about ways you need additional support. My hope for you is that you discover your needs and learn to communicate them in healthy ways. Finally, as a team member, you can consider how you might approach these issues when you become a manager yourself. Your struggles now can inspire a future career.

Team Leaders, I am selecting nuggets of wisdom to help you and your staff triumph over burnout. My hope for you is that you discover ways to feel good again, and as a result, enjoy greater performance. I also hope you model for your team the importance of self-care and take action in creating a Culture of Wellbeing in your organization.

Tips for Team Leaders

- On a scale from 1 to 10, consider what are your levels of exhaustion, cynicism, and ineffectiveness. What changes do you want to make, starting now? What resources do you have? Track your symptoms and note whether they're improving over time.

- Check in with your team. Are they experiencing symptoms of burnout? Remember that for people to share, you must first have earned their trust.

- Promote the wellbeing of all employees by improving the strategic-management issues that cause burnout, including overwork. Fully reject the outdated notion that we can do more with less, and make sure your employees have goals that are achievable, at a pace that's sustainable.

- When an employee quits, don't reassign his projects without fully understanding the existing workload of remaining employees. If you don't have the necessary people power, give yourself permission to adjust your goals and timelines.

- Revisit the ethics of labor laws. While salaried employees legally may work beyond 40 hours a week, is it ethical for leaders to expect this? Every human needs time to rejuvenate and create a vibrant life—and this makes us more creative and effective at work.

- Ask yourself: Do you most value your employees who work the longest hours, or those who produce the best results? Send your employees home and stop rewarding people who work late.

When we understand the debilitating costs of burnout on individuals as well as organizations, we can recognize the importance (and urgency!) of transformational change. This is a great foundation as we move forward to discuss the 10 Dimensions of Wellbeing that will help us to eradicate burnout.

We can do it!

3

DISCOVERING THE 10 DIMENSIONS OF WELLBEING

I wish I could tell you what it was like the day I finally resigned. I would like to share that my boss, Michelle, sat primly across from me at the small table in her office, not expecting the resignation letter I would coolly hand her. I would like to tell you that she looked displeased and bothered by my announcement, and that she didn't have the nerve to look me in the eye, because deep down she recognized she had treated me poorly. I want to explain to you that I felt relieved as the weight of those work responsibilities shifted from my shoulders and landed elsewhere. The day I quit is a critical piece of the story—and other than the sound of my blood pumping in my ears, I can't remember a thing.

Obviously, my stress that day frazzled my brain and clear memories aren't accessible. Also, this was an especially painful time, and after I quit, I began my long healing process back to wellbeing. I gave myself permission to not dwell on bad memories from work, and I began to focus instead on activities that made me feel good. My exploration of wellbeing was just beginning.

While I can't tell you about the distraught look on Michelle's face, I can share with you all the things I've learned since then. I discovered there are a multitude of ways we can take better care of our bodies, minds, and spirits, and I devised a framework to better understand how to recover from burnout—or better yet, how to avoid it entirely. I've grouped this knowledge into 10 Dimensions of Wellbeing, which I'm sharing with you in this chapter.

As you're reading, if you're pressed for time, you might be tempted to skip chapters. I totally get that desire to rush through, because of the weight of your responsibilities. Just remember that skipping chapters isn't ideal because I'm writing this book to help you absorb new concepts and ideas in each chapter. You deserve all the knowledge and helpful tips in these pages.

If you're a team member, it's helpful for you to understand all the dimensions, for your own benefit. Perhaps you can model wellbeing yourself! You have influence and sway, being exactly who you are. If the idea of putting your own needs first fills you with dread because of the culture at your work, then I encourage you to share this book with the leaders. Ask them to read it at the very least, and perhaps there can be an open conversation about the concepts, maybe in your workplace book club. In addition, you can help form a committee to discuss the wellbeing of the staff. You don't have control over how the leaders respond, but you are empowered to find the best work environment for you—one that cultivates wellbeing.

If you're a team leader, it's helpful for you to understand all the dimensions, for your own benefit. Also, where might your staff need extra support? Help them feel secure, valued, and respected as they learn to prioritize themselves. It's transformative at work when leaders model wellbeing for each other and for their teams. If this book resonates with you, consider sharing it with your work colleagues and including it in discussions of your office book club. In addition, you might lead a committee that delves into the wellbeing of the staff.

Here is a glimpse into the 10 Dimensions of Wellbeing. I'll go into greater detail about each one in upcoming chapters.

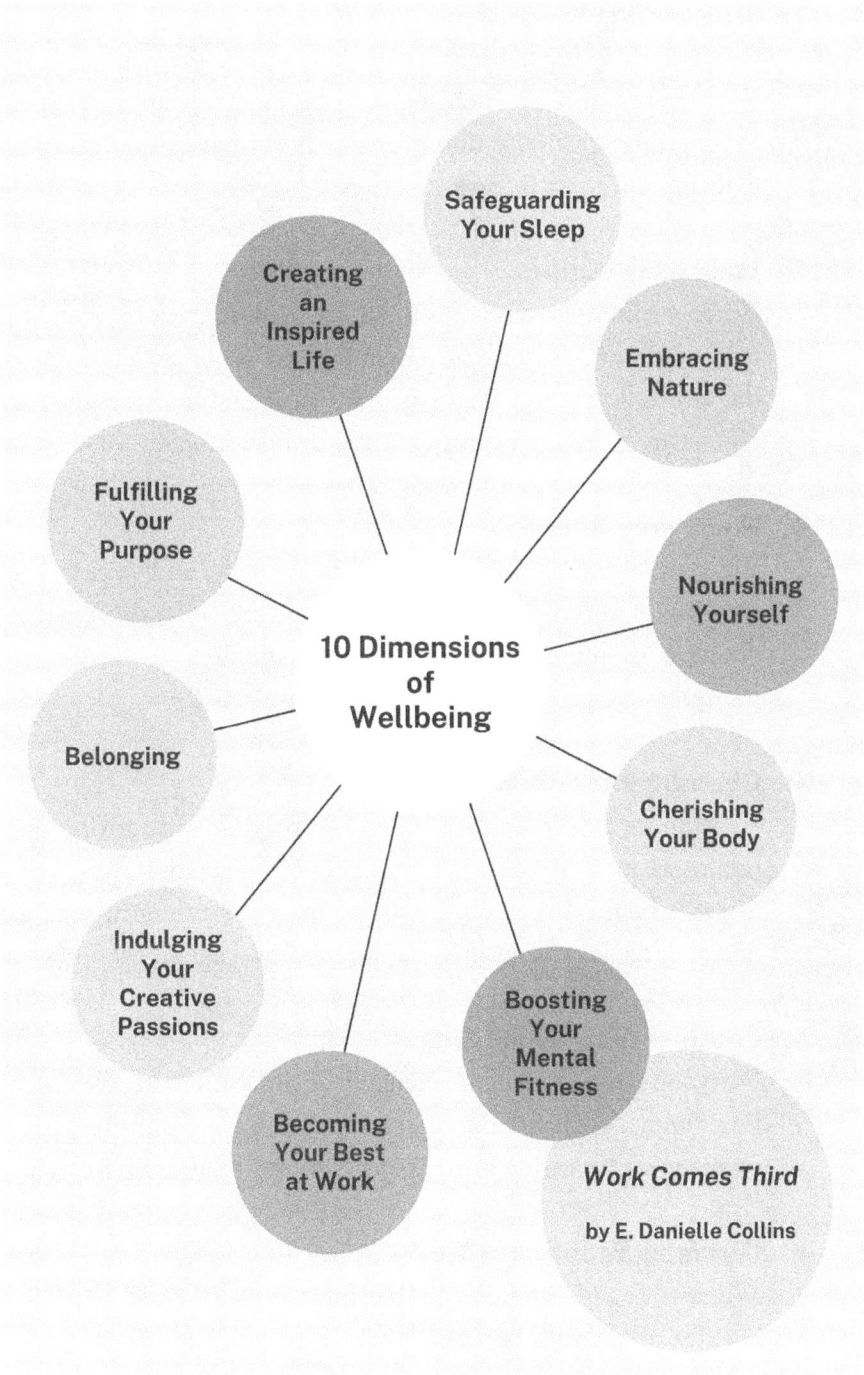

Safeguarding
Your Sleep

Creating
an
Inspired
Life

Embracing
Nature

Fulfilling
Your
Purpose

Nourishing
Yourself

10 Dimensions
of
Wellbeing

Belonging

Cherishing
Your Body

Indulging
Your
Creative
Passions

Boosting
Your
Mental
Fitness

Becoming
Your Best
at Work

Work Comes Third

by E. Danielle Collins

1. **Safeguarding Your Sleep**
   Good sleep is the cornerstone of our health. We need at least seven hours of sleep each night to be better decision-makers, enjoy greater creativity, and prevent a host of diseases, including diabetes and heart disease.

2. **Embracing Nature**
   When we immerse ourselves in nature, we lose track of time. We forget our worries from the past and let go of our anxieties about the future. As we experience awe, we transcend the moment and rejuvenate ourselves both physically and emotionally.

3. **Nourishing Yourself**
   What we consume impacts our bodies, minds, and spirits. The food we eat must nourish us and be sustainable. Likewise, the media we consume affects our world view, mindset, and resilience. It's never been more important that we use it as a force for good.

4. **Cherishing Your Body**
   It's time to rediscover the joy we had playing and moving our bodies as kids. It's also time to better protect ourselves from forever chemicals, which are found in everyday items, such as nonstick cookware, cosmetics, and food packaging.

5. **Boosting Your Mental Fitness**
   Everyone can become more mentally fit and learn to handle tough times with a positive mindset, rather than staying unhappy. Recognizing our uncaring inner voices is an important step forward.

6. **Becoming Your Best at Work**
   When you're at your best, you feel safe to be authentic. You have healthy boundaries between work and home, and you rejuvenate fully with healthy breaks and mandatory vacations.

7. **Indulging Your Creative Passions**

   When we give ourselves permission to express our creativity, we find ourselves in a state of blissful flow (coined by Mihaly Csikszentmihalyi) and we enjoy being completely immersed in a task. This is a powerful, healing dimension and we have an opportunity to discover more about our favorite pursuits.

8. **Belonging**

   When we belong, we feel valued and respected by our teammates, colleagues, and bosses, and we feel accepted for who we inherently are. The myth of the ideal employee, however, makes us feel like we can never measure up.

9. **Fulfilling Your Purpose**

   One of the keys to feeling happy at work is understanding our purpose. When our job reflects our values, and we understand how our work makes a difference, we're more likely to feel fulfilled.

10. **Creating an Inspired Life**

    We're equipped with a beautiful capacity for spirituality, and science is proving we enjoy greater optimism, resilience, and innovation when we're living a spiritual life. We'll explore how to build a life of fulfillment and meaning.

I'm a Certified Wellness Inventory Coach, and this intensive training helped me understand important concepts about the interconnection of the dimensions of our lives, as well as how to create a lifestyle built on healthy habits. Jim Strohecker, CEO of HealthWorld Online, and co-creator of the Wellness Inventory Certification Training, helped me experience my biggest aha moments. I want to thank and acknowledge the Wellness Inventory Certification Training for permission to share life-changing concepts.

> Burning out dramatically affects every area of our lives, from our sleep to our mental fitness.

I spent years wondering why my stress at work was seeping into my relationships, creative pursuits, and spiritual practices. I thought something was wrong with me because I struggled to keep work in its own box. Jim explained that all the areas of our lives affect the whole and impact each other.

When I developed the 10 Dimensions of Wellbeing to eradicate burnout, I purposefully included "Becoming Your Best at Work." Notice that this is just one dimension in our rich and colorful lives. Also notice that this dimension shares space with nine others, and that it doesn't take up all the room.

When we're chronically stressed at work, this negatively impacts all the other dimensions. Burning out dramatically affects every area of our lives, from our sleep to our mental fitness. When we feel stressed and overwhelmed the following can happen:

- Our sleep suffers.
- Our time in nature feels flat, as our sensory awareness is reduced.
- We eat quickly and we comfort ourselves with food and drink.
- Our addiction to doomscrolling compounds our misery.
- Our bodies weaken and age as we forget to move and have fun.
- We stay upset and reactive, dwelling in fear.
- We take our laptops on vacation and fail to rejuvenate.
- We have less energy for our favorite pastimes.
- Our ability to be authentic is wiped out, as we feel unsafe at work.
- We align ourselves with values that are not our own.
- We fail to say YES to life as we lose our connection to the greater whole.

And when these things happen, our level of resilience is diminished.

Fortunately, we can use these dimensions not just to understand the impact of burnout, but we can reflect on each dimension and discover ways to rally in the face of despair. I was so excited when Jim helped me understand that when you improve one area, you'll find some relief in the others as well.

Here's even more good news: you don't have to improve all of your dimensions all at once. *Whew!* Which of the dimensions are you most motivated to improve? Discover one or two that pique your interest and focus on those.

Loving the Small Steps

In our culture, we often think, *I've got to accomplish all these goals all at once or I have zero value as a human being.* Right? Go big or go home! This is a terrible myth that doesn't serve you. What's true is you need to choose small, doable goals, and acknowledge your progress along the way.

Dr. Robert Maurer wrote a fascinating book, *One Small Step Can Change Your Life: The Kaizen Way,* and he explains how we're not successful with sweeping changes because we set ourselves up to fail. "Kaizen" is the Japanese word for "good change" or "improvement," and it refers to the small, fun steps that are safe and easy to do.

These baby steps work well because we tiptoe around our amygdala, the part of the brain that resists change and launches us into fight or flight. The laughably small steps keep us from triggering that part of the brain. When you read the corresponding chapter for the dimension you're most excited to pursue, remember to take steps so small it might feel silly.

Understanding the Stages of Change

We think that change is like the show *I Dream of Jeannie*, where she simply blinks and magically the situation has transformed. If people want to change—then BLINK—they just have the willpower to do it instantly and permanently. Anything less is a sign of softness.

Eventually, our reserves of will power and grit run dry, and then we predictably stop meditating, or jogging, or eating salads. We feel shame for failing and then we let the new habit go. We don't understand that when we jump straight into action (BLINK!) we have skipped important stages to prepare us for change.

James Prochaska, PhD, asked the question, "What happens when people successfully change a behavior on their own?" He discovered that these folks went through many steps before actually making changes. He shared his Transtheoretical Model about the stages of change in our health behaviors, and transformed the way we look at everything from smoking cigarettes to using contraceptives.

In the earliest stage, people deny there's a problem, and they're not actively seeking professional help. Later, we recognize there is an issue, and we begin gathering information. As we decide to move forward, we make a plan and prepare for action within the next 30 days. Finally, we are ready to act! This is the stage most people understand when thinking about changing. It's an exciting place to be as we build momentum. BLINK! Ideally, people will sustain this change for a year or more.

It's normal for folks to experience obstacles and stop their new, healthy behaviors. At this point, people feel shame, and it's important they understand that change is not a straight-line process. We can exit and re-enter the previous stages of change. When we do cycle back, it's a great opportunity to learn about our habits and have fun with our steps forward. Having a good friend or coach to help when we relapse makes a difference in our success.

How ready are you for change? What stage best describes your current experience?

Discovering the Continuum of Wellbeing

We don't burn out overnight. It's a long process, day after day, of traveling the wrong direction on the continuum. Imagine a road and at one end is our total wellbeing of our minds, bodies, and spirits. We enjoy peak performance and our greatest fulfillment. What awaits us at the opposite end of the road? Chronic stress, burnout, disease, and ultimately, premature death.

Every morning, you have an opportunity to start your day at least facing the direction of wellbeing. You might even take a positive step forward, by choosing a healthy breakfast. Meditating and walking in nature can also jumpstart your days toward positivity. As you move through the morning, you may become troubled by alarming emails from your boss, difficult headlines, or an overwhelming to-do list. When you don't feel like you have control and experience a lack of autonomy, you may unwittingly begin facing the direction of burnout, and you can feel your emotions shifting from love to fear, as the weight of your responsibilities presses down on your body.

You have an opportunity throughout the day to recognize that unwelcome weight, and plant yourself again facing wellbeing. I understand now that when I left my office to call my friend from the car, this wasn't laziness—this was me trying to figure out, without the tools or vocabulary, how to turn myself around on the continuum. With rejuvenating breaks during the day, you have a chance to take steps toward fulfillment. On days when you instead sprint toward burnout, you have the opportunity to feel compassion for yourself at bedtime. And to dwell on the promise of a new day.

....

Tips for Team Leaders

- Consider a time when you successfully developed a new, healthy habit. What helped you to incorporate it into your lifestyle?

- After learning about the 10 Dimensions of Wellbeing, which one are you most excited about? Visualize yourself having fun exploring this dimension, and consider how your body, mind, and spirit will benefit. Remember that when you feel better in one dimension, all the others are positively impacted. Which dimensions are your staff most excited about?

- The stages of change help us properly prepare for taking transformative action. As you visualize yourself exploring one of the dimensions, where are you in the stages? No matter your response, acknowledge your new understanding and acceptance of the process.

- Pay attention to which direction you're facing on the continuum of wellbeing. Are you making small choices each day that lead you to greater health and happiness? Or are you madly striding in the opposite direction, toward burnout and premature death? When you model your healthy choices for your employees, they too will feel safe taking care of their own needs.

- Boost your resilience by taking regular breaks during the day, breathing deeply, eating healthy food, and moving your body! Create a lifestyle where you pursue your passions outside of work.

....

Learning about all the ways we can cherish ourselves is important. You are empowered to create the life you want, step by step. It's time to set down the burden of our sadness and hurt, and become curious about what changes we can make that lead us to fulfillment, meaning, and contribution. We'll begin with the first dimension and focus on the foundation of sleep.

We can do it!

4

SAFEGUARDING YOUR SLEEP

Steve woke early again. He rolled over, trying to fall back to sleep, but as usual, thoughts about work trickled into his consciousness. He could hear the soft breathing of his wife, Marissa, as she slept with her back turned to him. Steve was glad that both she and their five-year-old son were still asleep.

He knew he shouldn't check the time, but he couldn't help himself. Reaching over, he grasped his phone and felt his stomach lurch when he saw the screen. *Not again.* He only had two more hours until he was supposed to rise and begin his ambitious day at work. Steve's brain skipped ahead to the board meeting that would occur in a few hours, and he kicked himself for not sleeping longer.

As the executive director of a midsize nonprofit, Steve had so many responsibilities that he often felt exhausted. He had fleeting notions that maybe his staff was exhausted as well. This morning, his thoughts raced to his biggest concern—how to retain his employees.

"How can I keep Val and Jessie from quitting? What should I do? We can't afford to hire new people now," Steve grumbled to himself, and then he launched into serious stewing over the strategic plan and budget, worried that he and his team wouldn't make their goals if employees quit. Deep down, he despised this feeling of vulnerability and recognized he was desperate for his board's approval.

Steve also was beginning to recognize that his professional drive was squashing his family time, and that he had been short-tempered with his son yesterday. He felt a surge of guilt, so he threw off the covers and climbed out of bed, again starting his day hours early and filled with anxiety and shame.

Steve represents my clients who have struggled with sleep. They reached out, ready for change, and were able to deepen their purpose-filled work while also feeling more playful and lighthearted with their families.

I'm fortunate that (unlike Steve) safeguarding my sleep usually comes naturally for me. Despite grief, burnout, and heartbreak, I regularly sleep at least eight hours. What has kept me from sleeping? Recovering from shoulder surgery. For three months, I only slept a few hours at a time, carefully propped up on various pillows. My norm, however, is to sleep well, and I'm grateful for this. We all have a top dimension in our lives that is likely going smoothly. What dimension seems easier for you? We want to acknowledge what we're already doing well and focus on maintaining our efforts.

....

> Sleep is the foundation of our life. To be at our best, adults need a minimum of seven hours of high-quality sleep each night.

....

Not having enough sleep is a huge drain on our internal resources. Sometimes employees work late in the evenings, yet they're expected to be sitting at their desks first thing the next morning. They are physically there, tapping at the keyboard, but their minds are blurry and their spirits are dampened. They are far from their best.

Our culture rewards us for the number of hours we plug away at our projects. It's critical that at all times we be "busy," and we're rarely rewarded for our productivity and efficiency. If we were, we would be encouraged to go home earlier, spend time with our families, get a solid night's sleep—and arrive again the next day, refreshed and rejuvenated.

Sleep is the foundation of our life. To be at our best, adults need a minimum of seven hours of high-quality sleep each night, according to the US Centers for Disease Control and Prevention (CDC).

What happens when we shortchange ourselves? Nothing good. Impacts of poor sleep include the following:

- Reduced work efficiency
- Reduced decision-making skills
- Slower than normal reaction time
- Loss of motivation
- Poor memory
- Reduced concentration
- Mood fluctuations

Sounds fun, right? Our bodies suffer as well, and the costs from long-term sleep deprivation are staggering. Not getting enough sleep over time puts us at greater risk of these conditions:

- Alzheimer's
- Diabetes
- Heart disease
- Obesity
- Breast cancer
- Accelerated aging

Lack of good sleep is the harbinger for deteriorating health; our relationships with our inner circle suffer, and we're less productive at work.

The Cycle of Insomnia

Sleep is serious business! Many folks struggle with insomnia and find that when they wake up, they can't go back to sleep. In fact, the more they focus on their insomnia, the more anxious they feel, and the harder it is to let go and drift away. Some sleep experts encourage you to leave your bed if you can't control your mind chatter and stop worrying about the important day ahead. I encourage you to think about what is true for you. There are ways we can be in the present moment that are helpful, even in the middle of the night.

I have created a realm for sleeping and I've told my mind that this time is not for problem-solving or planning. Only for rejuvenating sleep. When I do wake in the middle of the night, I try not to think about my problems, and instead I focus on the present moment. I took yoga for over five years from the same instructor, and I can still hear her voice in my head, walking us through Savasana, a final relaxation so wonderful that we didn't even notice the hard floors and tired bodies. She told us to relax our toes, feet, and ankles. Then relax our calves and knees and thighs—and we relaxed all our muscles, all the way up to the top of our heads. Imagining her voice is my go-to in the middle of the night and I rarely even make it to my fingers and arms. It keeps me from devolving into frustration and self-recrimination for not falling asleep sooner.

How can you create your own realm of sleep? When you wake, how do you soothe yourself and stay in the present moment? It's important to respect that we all have individual variations of what helps us drift back to sleep. You might slow your breath, express gratitude, or pray for the willingness to let go. Rather than fighting our loss of sleep, we can reframe it by gently telling ourselves, "Even if I'm not asleep, I can enjoy deeply resting."

If these moments of mindfulness aren't enough for you to drift off, you may need something else to focus on that won't remind you of work—perhaps a book that's not super-exciting and doesn't demand your attention. Furthermore, tracking your sleep with a wearable device can become a source of pressure, in the same way that seeing the face of your clock or phone makes you anxious there's only one hour left.

We create a negative cycle when we wake and then worry about our lack of sleep and not performing well at work the next morning. It's worth it to consider the deeper reasons for our anxiety—perhaps a sense of perfectionism or low self-esteem. We also all have internal critics that judge our accomplishments and fret about disappointing our team, and we'll dive deeply into these unhelpful voices in Chapter 8 – Boosting Your Mental Fitness.

There are concrete steps we can take to set ourselves up for the best sleep possible. Below are seven suggestions.

Seven Sleepytime Tips

1. Remove all screens from the bedroom.

    Yep, this is for real and it's a bit of a bummer. Research shows that screens inhibit the deep sleep our bodies need. Keep your laptop in your study, watch TV in your den, read a real book instead of your ipad, and charge your phone in another room.

    But my phone is my alarm clock, you say. Companies still make alarm clocks. Take care to position your clock so you can't see the time if you wake in the middle of the night.

    If removing all screens is too brutal, consider turning off all screens 90 minutes before bedtime to avoid the negative effects on your melatonin, a sleep hormone. In addition, either turn off your phone or set it on *do not disturb*, so that the reminders and notifications don't disrupt your sleep.

2. Go to sleep and wake up at regular times—even on the weekends.

    This one is tough for me, being an uber night owl who wants to stay up late on weekends. But for folks who suffer from insomnia, keeping the same hours strengthens your circadian rhythm.

3. Use your bed for all good things—sleep, sex, soothing music, and perhaps some meditation and reflections of gratitude.

    If you have to work at home in the evenings, do it anywhere but in your bed. Keep all work materials out of your bedroom.

4. Make your bedroom your sanctuary—cozy, comfortable, and quiet.

    Soothing colors like blues and greens make us feel peaceful, while lined curtains keep out unwanted light from streetlamps. If your sweetie snores, consider ear plugs or a sleep machine that gently drowns out ambient noise. Should your partner have sleep apnea or other disorders that keep you from a good night's sleep, consider separate bedrooms. Many couples try this on a temporary basis and then find they need the nighttime space to be less tired and irritable during the day. When we can escape binary thinking (couples are supposed to sleep together) we discover many different options that may serve us better.

5. Think twice about what you put in your body.

    Stop drinking coffee at least six to seven hours before bedtime.

    Because alcohol is a sedative, people think it helps them to sleep. This is a common misunderstanding, and while alcohol may initially put people into a heavy sleep, it also fragments our sleep, causing us to wake up easily, many times throughout the night. In addition, alcohol blocks your dream sleep, which we need for healthy brains.

    Likewise, sleeping pills may sedate us, but this is not sleep. Some are habit-forming and are meant only for short-term use. Neither sleeping pills nor alcohol have the restorative benefits of natural sleep.

6. If you're stewing over something and can't stop, consider using a "Worry Book" or a "God Box."

   Write down your concerns and fears, then close the book or shut the box. It's time to let it go, at least for the moment. The universe can handle it while you sleep.

7. You'll enjoy deeper sleep if you exercise regularly.

   Make sure you stop exercising at least three hours before you go to bed.

These seven tips will improve your sleep, but if you want to really increase your productivity, consider a nap in the early afternoon. Yes, a lovely, delicious, 20-minute power nap.

Enjoy a Power Nap!

We sleep in five stages that recur throughout the night. The beauty of a power nap is that it includes just the first two (be sure to set an alarm so you don't slip into deeper stages of sleep). Benefits include an increase in productivity, alertness, and stamina. People also experience improved memory and learning, as well as less stress.

Without a nap, your brain activity declines. By the end of the day, you may be pushing through projects, feeling depleted. You end up working longer hours, thinking you're accomplishing more—when in fact you would be more effective if you took a break and rejuvenated.

If taking a real nap seems unacceptable in your workplace, you have options. Close your door and turn out the lights, resting in your chair for a few minutes. In a cubicle, you can close your eyes and focus on deep breaths. Another option is to rest in your car during your lunch break.

Remember that taking a nap doesn't mean you're lazy—instead, it means you want to feel good, and also to deliver meaningful work in a timely manner for your organization. You want to be MORE productive, not less.

· ·

Tips for Team Leaders

- Consider how you can create a realm of sleep where analysis and planning are not allowed. Then get a good night's sleep yourself, for your own benefit as well as for your team.

- Consider: Do you most value your employees who work the longest hours, or those who produce the greatest results?

- Encourage your employees to minimize their overtime, and allow them to sleep in the morning following evening events.

- Take power naps or restful breaks, modeling for your employees how to rejuvenate during the day.

· ·

When folks say, "I'll sleep when I'm dead," we can help them understand that we value sleep and that by taking care of this basic necessity, we hope to forestall an early exit from this life. You deserve to live a healthier, longer, and more meaningful life—and sleep helps make that a reality.

We can do it!

5

EMBRACING NATURE

My dog, Boo, scampered with me on the wet sand, where the land intersects the sea. Years before, we had taught each other to play "This Way!" and it involved Boo chasing me madly in a grassy field, and then I'd change direction without warning and call out, "This way, my wild Boo, come this way!" and she charged after me once again. Boo was at her best in these moments, as she was off leash and free. She lost her mind in happiness when we played This Way by the ocean.

I played our favorite game as long as I could, until my legs and lungs cried out for rest. Then I slowed to a walk to catch my breath, and came to a stop by my husband. Boo joined us, with a giant smile on her face and ears alert and excited. My husband clipped her long leash back on and tied it around his waist; we thought she was settling back into a restrained existence.

Both my husband and I enjoy photography, and we pulled out our cameras to capture the foggy coast in Oregon. I shot photos of Haystack Rock, a monolithic sea stack along the shoreline, and then returned my camera to my backpack. Boo, still gleeful, began dragging us into the surf. Then she circled the two of us, wrapping her leash around our legs. As a wave rolled in, we tried running the other direction, but discovered we were tied together and we all fell into the ocean, laughing uncontrollably. Boo danced in the water with us, so delighted by her own mischief.

I remember a woman, sporting a big hat, was walking her well-behaved dog, and the woman had stopped in her tracks to laugh with us.

In that moment, I was the happiest I've ever been. This was my version of heaven, frolicking on a misty coast with my beloved border collie. As I write these words, I'm filled with joy and sadness. Joy because I'm so lucky to have this memory, and sadness that Boo has since died and my husband has moved out. I comfort myself, knowing that one day I'll return Boo's ashes to the Oregon coast, the place where she was her most exuberant self. I also comfort myself by focusing on my sweet Scout, a border collie I recently adopted from a rescue in Utah.

The happiest moment of my life, so far, took place in nature. It was supercharged by the sound of the waves, the sight of the sea stack, the briny smell of the ocean, and the feel of wet sand under my feet as Boo and I scampered together. The three of us were completely immersed in the moment, and there was no room for worries about the past or anxiety about the future. While my work responsibilities played no role whatsoever in the creation of my happiest time, sharing that moment with my inner circle imprinted it in my mind and connected me to something greater. Being in nature was transcendent.

> We are not meant to be an indoor species.

Our Bodies Love Being in Nature

The US Environmental Protection Agency found that we spend 87 percent of our time in enclosed buildings, and 6 percent of our time in our vehicles. *Ugh.* We spend so much time indoors that we forget our connection to nature. We are not meant to be an indoor species—we are designed to commune with vibrant landscapes and the wildlife that call them home.

Our bodies are healthier after we spend time in nature. We enjoy a decrease in our high blood pressure and are at a lower risk for strokes. Our sleep improves and we boost our immunity. Green spaces are important, and our long-term exposure could add 2.5 years to our lives.

Our mental fitness improves as well. When we're in nature, we intuitively understand that we feel better, as our mood lightens and our anxiety subsides. You won't be surprised to learn that scientific research has linked our time in nature with lower levels of stress hormones. In fact, spending just 20 to 30 minutes in nature showed the biggest drop in cortisol levels. In addition to decreased stress and anxiety, we enjoy greater focus, as well as a boost to our resilience as we ruminate less.

> We are designed to commune with vibrant landscapes and the wildlife that call them home.

Nature is our antidote for anxiety, including eco-anxiety (our fear that the climate crisis will cause suffering in our own lives). Having fled the smoke and wildfires on the West Coast, I understand well this fear, and I use it to shape my biggest decisions, including where to live, how to keep myself safe, etc. How can we balance our concerns for our environment—which is impacted every day by the carbon emissions, plastic, and forever chemicals created by humans—with our hope for the future?

Birds may be part of the answer!

Celebrating Birds

I came into this world loving dogs unconditionally, and my love for our feathered friends is different. It began slowly, with hints of pleasure as I watched them flit and flutter from one tree branch to the next. Over time I've become much more curious, wanting to identify them and understand their chirps. My love grew as I watched doves choose our back porch, year after year, to lay their eggs and feed their hatchlings. Now I feed a variety of birds each day, and one of my favorite sounds in the world is the sweet *chick-a-dee-dee-dee* that some twitter in happiness as they eat.

The birds are there, waiting for us to appreciate their mysterious ways. I always feel better after interacting with them or watching them from a window, so I wasn't surprised to learn that when we see or hear birds, it boosts our mental fitness, and this sense of wellbeing endures for hours!

Unfortunately, almost one-third of adult birds have disappeared in North America. That's three billion birds. Yes, *billion.* These birds are literally the canaries in the coal mine, warning us about the dire costs of habitat loss as humans claim more and more land for themselves. Birds are critical to dispersing seeds and fertilizing plants and flowers, and with their decline we could expect less flora, including trees and vegetables.

It is not too late, however. The North American Wetlands Conservation Act has helped increase the population of migratory birds, and it has had such a positive impact that we could use this approach with other birds. With additional habitat conservation measures, we can help the 70 percent of the remaining birds to hasten a resurgence.

How can we better appreciate the birds in our corner of the world?

- Pay attention and notice! You'll begin to recognize their chirps and songs.
- Explore smartphone apps such as Merlin Bird ID and BirdNet Sound ID (from the Cornell Lab of Ornithology) to identify the bird. You can also buy local guidebooks with photos.
- Provide clean drinking water, especially if it's below freezing.
- Once you understand which birds visit your backyard, provide healthy and appropriate food for them. I loved visiting the local bird store and learning more about the best foods at different

times of the year. I quickly realized I also needed a metal baffle to deter the squirrels from the feeder. I'm committed to feeding the birds and providing water throughout the seasons.
- Donate regularly to your favorite environmental organization.
- Join a birding group and meet other like-minded folks!
- Vote for leaders who will enact the needed conservation measures to protect the birds.

Immersing Ourselves in Nature

Exploring local, state, and national parks is a fun way to check out the different birds and to enjoy hiking in beautiful landscapes. Recognizing nature's role in improving our wellbeing, health care providers in both the US and Canada are now **prescribing visits to nature**, an exciting shift from telling patients to simply "exercise more." People who experience nature are more likely to safeguard it from the climate crisis.

In addition to prescribing nature, we're enjoying **forest bathing** as well. The Japanese practice is called "shinrin-yoku" and it describes being in the present moment, fully aware of your senses while enjoying nature. The purpose of forest bathing differs from other activities. For example, the objective of a brisk walk may be to count your steps and move your body outside. The objective of a hike is to reach your destination. The objective of forest bathing, however, is to leave behind the stress of work and to move slowly, appreciating what you can see, hear, and touch.

The next time you're immersed in nature, remember that it's a digital detox and sensory experience. Turn off your phone and find a place to sit quietly to focus on what you see. What colors pop? What shapes do you notice? Watch the leaves above gently move against the blue sky. Then focus on what you hear. Focus first on the sound that is furthest away. Then pay attention to the closest sound. Notice if some sounds make you feel more peaceful. Inhale deeply and pay attention to what you smell. How would you describe the air? Bend over and gently touch the ground near your shoe. Notice the texture as well as the temperature. What about this scene fills you with awe?

When we're bathing in our forest, we experience a boost to our immunity, with a higher number of natural killer cells (white blood cells that fight tumors). Japan registers its official trails by vetting them to ensure there are no pollutants in the locales, and shinrin-yoku is covered by insurance.

When we're in nature, we worry less about the past. We also can set our fears about the future aside, and by doing so, we become even more resilient. Mindfulness is at the heart of our resilience to stress. We can practice mindfulness in nature, with intention, and these rituals (such as breathing exercises, sensory experiences, and meditation) are great ways to appreciate the present moment and feel lighter. In addition, we ultimately better handle challenges at work.

Calming Your Mind with Your Breath

Enjoying gorgeous landscapes gives us the opportunity to experience awe, as well as to breathe deeply. Our breath is a powerful way we can bring energy and oxygen into our bodies, yet we're not good at breathing. We forget to breathe deeply, or we wear tight-fitting clothes, or we hunch over our keyboards. No one taught us to focus on our breathing.

However you're sitting (or sprawling), take a moment now to sit straight in your chair, and put your feet flat on the floor.

- Close your eyes.
- Breathe through your nose, with your mouth closed.
- Inhale deeply, allowing your abdomen and chest to expand. Keep inhaling as your collarbones lift.
- Pause, but don't hold your breath.

- Exhale slowly and fully, releasing your shoulders and then allowing your abdomen to contract.
- Notice how much better you feel!

Our breath affects our wellbeing. The calmer our breath, the calmer our mind, and the better we feel. This works in reverse as well (the calmer our mind, the calmer our breath) so when we're stressed, scared, or grieving, we may discover our breathing is restricted.

I found this out firsthand when I visited my massage therapist during a breakup with my boyfriend at the time. Heartsick, I rested face down on the table. While I enjoyed her efforts, I was still enveloped in sadness, and after the massage, I wanted her reassurance that I would heal, body and soul.

"How do you think my body and muscles are right now?" I asked.

She didn't miss a beat. "You've forgotten to breathe."

That's weird, I thought. Was she right? I focused on my rib cage, and realized it was barely expanding and contracting. I felt like a vice grip was on my chest, refusing to let me breathe deeply. I inhaled and exhaled purposefully on my drive home and began my journey to healing.

When we breathe deeply and smoothly, with intention, we energize our cells with oxygen and give our organs and muscles the opportunity to be at their best. If we're feeling overwhelmed, breathing deeply will translate into many healthy things for our bodies, minds, and spirits, which are all linked.

In my Wellness Inventory Certification Training, we learned about a soothing breathing ritual that I share with people attending my presentations.

It's easier for us to create new habits if we can fit them into our routine. When I wash my hands, I take long, deep breaths, inhaling and exhaling slowly. I linger by the sink, enjoying the bubbles and smelling the soap. You can try this too. If you do, leave the sink after you've enjoyed four to five deep breaths, letting everything else fall away.

Tips for Team Leaders

- Think of your happiest moments in life. Where did they take place? How can you bring more of that into your life? Consider how to communicate this with your team and encourage them to share, if you have a foundation of trust.

- When team members are working hard and are overwhelmed, "prescribe nature" and give them time off to visit their favorite, local green spaces. (Make sure to save a prescription for yourself!) Encourage everyone to share their experiences in the next staff meeting.

- If you or your staff experience eco-anxiety, give your staff time off to volunteer with their favorite environmental organization. You can also participate in walks and runs as a team, and raise money for everything from rebuilding the local trails to implementing conservation measures.

- When you're stressed and want to calm your mind, inhale to the count of four, and exhale to the count of eight. This keeps you feeling peaceful and mentally sharp.

- Use Post-it Notes with reminders and visibly display them at home or in your office. Every time you see one, deeply breathe. I have a pink one in my bathroom that says "Breathe Dani!"

- Remember that some mindfulness programs offered by companies shift the responsibility onto the individual employee, rather than addressing the systemic dysfunction and unfair conditions. Become an advocate for your team and address the toxic culture.

- Respect that our planet breathes too and weigh your decisions about the size of your carbon footprint at work. Then consider the impact of your personal activities.

••

When we embrace nature, we discover that it is part of who we fundamentally are. Being in nature helps us to thrive physically, mentally, and emotionally, and we must find ways to enjoy our favorite scenery even more. We need our leaders and policymakers to understand that when our natural landscapes are desecrated, our wellbeing suffers. We are nature, and nature is us, and what happens to our favorite green spaces impacts us as well. Nature is as essential to our lives as safe streets and running water.

We can do it!

6

NOURISHING YOURSELF

Ask yourself the following:

- When was the last time you ate in your car while commuting? How often do you eat fast food? Do you remember tasting or enjoying the food, or did it serve as basic sustenance?
- After a stressful day at work, do you unwind with alcohol? Are your glasses of wine getting bigger and bigger?
- Do you fill the quiet moments of your day by doomscrolling on social media?
- How often do you work through your lunch? You have a deadline, and work becomes more important than basic sustenance.
- When you're exhausted from work, do you use vaping or pot to soothe yourself?
- Do you find yourself too tired in the evenings to shop for groceries or pack a healthy lunch for the next day? Work has worn you out. You do manage to check your social media accounts, however, to make sure enough followers are liking your latest posts.

I get it. I have done many of these things myself.

Now I can see that they didn't work for me, and instead pushed me down a slippery path toward feeling chronically overwhelmed. I wasn't nourishing my body, mind, or soul, so how could I be at my best?

In this chapter, we're going to discuss two important ways we must nourish ourselves: feeding our bodies with nutritious food, and then feeding our minds by using social media as a force for good.

As adults, we're all responsible for the food we ingest and headlines we absorb. We're also responsible for including in our schedules things we deem important. When did it become acceptable for eating to not be a priority? It's a fundamental life process.

Let's discuss three intriguing ideas I learned from my Wellness Inventory Certification Training.

Three Tips for Mindful Eating

1. Pay attention to **WHAT** you eat.

    Let's talk about the importance of organic, whole foods. What does it mean when our food is organic? It's a label for produce and grains that were grown with natural fertilizers, in ways that protect the soil and water. It's also a label used for meat, dairy, and eggs that protects animal welfare. The animals roamed freely outdoors and weren't given growth hormones or antibiotics.

    The less pesticides and growth hormones in our food, the better. Likewise, the more humanely we treat animals, the better. I began eating organic dairy products years ago. When I learned about the Dirty Dozen, an annual list of veggies and fruits that are the most contaminated with pesticides and should be avoided, I began buying organic produce as well. My food journey has evolved, and now I buy organic products as much as possible, and I choose my grocery store based on the availability of these foods. This is a personal choice and it isn't cheap, but it's become a priority for me.

I'm now a pescatarian as well, and this means I eat fish but not other meat. Again, my food journey throughout the decades began in my 20s when I didn't enjoy eating beef anymore. Years later, I drove past a truck taking chickens to be slaughtered, and I never ate chicken again. Likewise, I watched a crab die on the shore, and was done eating crab and lobster. I don't like the effect of dairy on my body and no longer drink milk. Our food choices are deeply personal and reflect our values. I spend time figuring out how to get enough protein, fiber, and calcium. I share all this not because you should follow my path, but to help you consider your own choices. How has your own food journey evolved?

Decades ago, experts recommended that if our bodies were fat, we should cut out the fat from our diets. Turns out this was not accurate, and the culprit is likely sugar, not fat. So I'm super-cautious about diet recommendations. Recent research found that those who ate right had a lower chance of contracting COVID-19. ("Eating right" meant a diet heavy on fruits, vegetables, nuts, and olive oil, with some fish and poultry, and only small amounts of red meat—the equivalent of the Mediterranean Diet.) Likewise, a new study found that when folks ate fruits, vegetables, beans, nuts, whole grains, and olive oil, with modest amounts of meat, they had a lower risk of early death— plus the benefit of their diet having a smaller environmental footprint. This Planetary Health Diet is adaptable to different cultural preferences.

Both the Mediterranean Diet and the Planetary Health Diet focus on eating whole foods. What are whole foods? They are unprocessed food that comes directly from plants and animals, such as fruits and vegetables. Both diets also limit our consumption of ultra-processed foods, which is vital for our health.

What are ultra-processed foods? Unfortunately, our modern American diet relies heavily on these industrially manufactured foods, with nearly 60 percent of our daily calories coming from them. In most cases, the vitamins, minerals, and fiber are stripped from these "foods" and replaced by additives and artificial ingredients. Examples of these foods include sugary breakfast cereals, potato chips, hot dogs, sodas, doughnuts, and frozen meals. These foods are often high in added sugar and saturated fat, which are ingredients we should limit. Manufacturers purposefully stimulate cravings and overeating by chemically manipulating these products.

You won't be surprised to learn that research shows a direct association between eating large amounts of these ultra-processed foods and serious health issues, including early death, dementia, cancer, and a host of other problems. Even ultra-processed *plant* foods increase the risk of heart attacks. Ultra-processing is uniquely damaging to our food and health. While we won't be able to eliminate these foods completely from our diet, we can take steps to reduce our exposure:

- Choose whole foods, such as fruits and vegetables. If they're not available, consider foods that have been minimally modified, such as frozen vegetables.
- Pay attention to where you're shopping in the grocery store. The fresh items are often along the perimeter, while the ultra-processed foods are in the middle.
- Read the ingredients list to determine if it's made from real food.
- Drink more water and less soda.

What one healthy ingredient would you have fun introducing into your diet? Here's an important tip to developing new eating habits: initially, focus on adding healthy food rather than eliminating longtime favorites. Focus on pleasure and satiety, and give yourself permission to change your eating habits over time.

2. Pay attention to **HOW** you eat.

    Do you eat standing over the sink? Or at your desk? Or in your car? Compare how different it feels to instead dine at a gorgeous table, with music and candlelight. This is a stretch at work, so try to leave your desk and go to the breakroom or eat outside at a picnic table.

    Be present and notice the food on your plate, including its color and texture. Eat slowly and savor each bite, using your senses to fully enjoy each moment. Every time we eat is an opportunity to feel gratitude for whoever prepared our meal (including ourselves!).

    In addition, when we consider how we eat, we can pay attention to the order that we eat the food on our plate. Research has found that "meal sequencing" helps us to feel fuller longer and to eat less. If you're like me, you eat the tastiest morsels first, perhaps the bread and butter, or maybe the pasta. This fills my belly with high-glycemic carbs that spike blood sugar levels. Hmm . . .

    When we eat vegetables, proteins, and fat at the beginning of our meal, and we eat the refined carbohydrates like rice and bread last, our blood sugar levels improve, and we feel satiated. This is a great first step to eating mindfully, because you don't have to radically change your meals.

3. Pay attention to **WHY** you eat.

    If we're lucky, we're eating to maintain an optimal level of energy and health.

    Eating is also aligned with our values. We may choose to enjoy a vegetarian, or vegan, or organic meal. It feels good when we live by our values, and it gives meaning to our dining experience.

    At times, we eat for comfort. The pandemic is in the rear-view mirror, but its impact lingers, as it turned our lives upside down. In addition, our country is deeply divided and the headlines are frightening. Finally, all of us are personally struggling, either with a relationship, our health, or our finances. While we may be stressed and emotional from our challenges at work, we're also troubled in other areas of our lives. In trying our best to cope, most of us have imbibed in a substance seeking comfort, whether we're treating ourselves to potato chips or drinking our favorite brew. Let's have a ton of self-compassion and recognize our current state of distress.

Let's also not turn these moments of seeking comfort into habits that don't serve us, creating a lifestyle based on addiction and self-medication, rather than wellbeing. Alcohol consumption and cigarette smoking are risk factors for cancer, not to mention the emotional toll on our loved ones. I've watched from a distance as alcoholism devastates my family, from one generation to the next. Two cousins have died, and who knows how many relatives are continuing to deny their own addiction.

People are familiar with the dangers of alcohol and cigarette smoking, but folks often think that smoking pot is harmless. Research, however, shows a range of health problems, including higher risk for heart attacks and strokes. In addition, marijuana products are much more potent than they used to be, with little oversight.

I understand well your desire to numb your pain. I urge you to seek help—from your best friend, from an AA meeting, from your therapist, from whomever you can trust who wants what is best for you. You are loved, and you deserve this.

In addition to consuming fewer addictive substances, we're at our best when we feed our minds positive news and uplifting narratives. It's our responsibility to find our news from responsible sources, recognize disinformation, and refuse to spread it. Let's talk about social media!

Five Ways to Use Social Media as a Force for Good

1. Embrace authenticity.

    Posts that are authentic share more than the rehearsed selfies (with breasts and butt provocatively positioned) and gleeful tales of travel (that disregard the long airport lines and crowded tourist destinations).

    Instead, authentic posts include our own personal stories that help our friends understand our lives aren't perfect. We demonstrate our resilience and show there is value in our struggle.

    Images can also be more authentic. They're taken during real-life moments, not recreated for Instagram. Also, you're not missing these real-life events, such as your baby's first steps, in an attempt to capture an image for social media.

2. Gain awareness of your emotions.

    When we're in the present moment, we can see how social media affects our emotions and our bodies.

    Consider your intentions as you open your favorite social media site. Are you wanting to connect with your community? Or are you distracting yourself from something in real life? Now pay attention to your emotions as you scroll. Where in your body do you feel it? Think through how, or if, you want to respond. Choosing the path that helps you enjoy a sense of equilibrium is best.

> Long ago, I stopped buying fashion magazines because their unwelcome subtext was that I wasn't enough, exactly the way I am. In a similar way, I now limit my time on social media.

I realized early on that I felt unsettled after reading certain posts, like how I used to feel after seeing the ads and articles in women's magazines—uncomfortable and vaguely anxious. Long ago, I stopped buying fashion magazines because their unwelcome subtext was that *I wasn't enough, exactly the way I am.* In a similar way, I now limit my time on social media.

I believe that you'll also be able to make better choices about how often to visit different sites, and the specific ways that you want to interact, as you become more aware of your emotions and the impact on your body.

3. Share portrayals of hope.

    Are you sharing posts that will inspire, encourage, and motivate? In a world where 24-hour news spews images of suffering around the world, how can we promote kindness and integrity?

    Witnessing acts of goodness helps us to feel connected to each other. Witnessing acts of violence creates distance.

    Research shows that portrayals of hope and gratitude have a high likelihood of being shared—inspiring posts can go viral as well!

4. Recognize disinformation and conspiracy theories and refuse to share them.

    Our country is bitterly divided, and for us to unite, we need to once again share a common reality. Right now, a substantial number of voters exist in a fundamentally different media ecosystem, where false and menacing information is widely spread on social media platforms. As humans, when we don't question conspiracy theories, it's often because we want them to be true, as these theories align with our point of view. Furthermore, Big Tech uses addictive algorithms of hate, and they have harmed the mental fitness of our kids.

It has been a murky and challenging situation for everyone, and now we've added artificial intelligence to the social media mix. No photo or video can be trusted. Furthermore, AI is being developed using the copyrighted works of authors, without their permission or compensation. No, I'm not a fan. Wealthy companies don't get to steal our intellectual property.

Let's consider the continuum of wellbeing that we discussed in Chapter 3 – Discovering the 10 Dimensions of Wellbeing. Regardless of who we voted for, we've all felt anger and disbelief while scrolling (and the companies count on our outrage to keep us hooked on their sites). When we share the post without thinking, we stay stuck in our anger, and we march ourselves toward the despair and disease that lead to premature death. When we work through our emotions and remember that we want to be a force for good, then we feel joy and excitement as we share stories of hope. We stride toward greater wellbeing.

Big Tech continues to abdicate their fact-checking responsibilities. Now, more than ever, we must pause before hitting the share button and confirm the authenticity of the post. In the morass that is now social media, we need trusted sources of legitimate news organizations that vet these photos and videos for us. We can support these individual organizations that use their resources to ensure we read more accurate news. We can also use tools like Apple News, which shares headlines from trustworthy sources.

You can help reduce the spread of disinformation. Ask yourself questions like these:

Who benefits from sharing false narratives?
Is it so salacious that it's probably clickbait?
Why do I want to share this post? How am I making the world better?
Is the web address real? Or is it designed to appear real to fool me?
Is the information also on reputable news sites?

Fact-checking websites are a great place to probe further. Here are some options:

- MediaBiasFactCheck.com
- FactCheck.org
- PolitiFact.com
- Snopes.com

5. Limit your screen time.

Staying constantly connected leads to overwhelm and burnout. In fact, people are now addicted to their phones and social media. Taking a break from our screens helps us to rejuvenate and to connect with each other in real life.

The content of what you consume on your screens matters, and social media is particularly problematic. In addition, excessive time spent on social media impacts our wellbeing. As adults, we should limit our social media time to 30 to 60 minutes a day, according to research by Melissa Hunt at the University of Pennsylvania. Remember how important it is to model healthy use of your smartphone for your kids and coworkers.

What do you think of the following ideas?

- Always keep your phone away from the meal table.
- Turn off your phone in the evening.
- Keep screens away from babies. Create a contract with your teen about acceptable use of their smartphone.
- Turn off your phone so the notifications don't disturb your sleep.
- Take the weekends off from social media and the news.
- Enjoy a tech-free vacation, leaving behind your screens—and your work!

I challenge you to not grab your phone during the empty spaces of your life. As you wait for your doctor's appointment, focus on your breath rather than checking your social media. Sit in the airport with your phone in your pocket and people-watch instead. Listen closely to your friend when you're on a bus ride together. See your dog delight in your attention when you walk her without wearing earbuds or checking your phone. One of the most important outcomes of limiting screen time is that we can deepen our connections with our favorite people. And dogs!

Tips for Team Leaders

- Remember that it's often easier to add a healthy item into our meals rather than to eliminate something. What nutritious food would you enjoy introducing into your diet? This is a fun way to begin your journey back to healthy eating.

- Offer fresh fruit for employees in the breakroom as a healthy change from the candy machine.

- Avoid "phubbing" your employees! Phubbing is an unfortunate phenomenon where you snub the people who are in your presence and instead use your phone. We tell ourselves no one cares, but they do, and research shows phubbing makes people feel unheard.

- During meaningful conversations, keep your phone out of sight. Just having the phone on the table, not even in use, reduces empathy and trust. With this in mind, make your staff meetings phone-free.

Taking small steps each day helps us to change our eating habits over time, as we seek to eat more whole foods and less that are ultra-processed. Taking small steps as we learn to use social media as a force for good is also critical to our success. When we nourish our bodies and minds alike, we enjoy greater wellbeing.

We can do it!

7

CHERISHING YOUR BODY

As I prepared to do the headstand, I calmly stood on my blue yoga mat in the back row, nestled between muscular men. My instructor walked us through the pose, and I got on all fours, clasped my fingers together, and then rocked forward, jutting my hips in the air while my hands cushioned and stabilized my head. I swung my legs upward, gently teetered, and finally found my balance upside down.

With satisfaction, I closed my eyes because I wanted to bring my focus inward. I also knew that not everyone could do the headstand, and that those of us in the pose were likely getting stares from others; I didn't want to worry about my wobbles. As much as possible, I kept my eyes shut.

I heard the man on my right come out of the pose, resting his body on the floor. The one on the left never tried and remained flat on his back, in corpse position. It struck me that I could do things with my body that men couldn't do, and I almost giggled out loud in delight. This had never before been my reality. My random and entertaining thoughts reminded me that my ego was still part of my practice.

I'm not a joiner, so when I began attending yoga class, I surprised myself. I wanted to see if it was a good fit for my body and temperament, and it turns out that during those years, before bone spurs and shoulder surgeries, I became quite the yogini. Who knew? I found my instructor's voice to be distinct and soothing, as she walked us through the asanas that began with sun salutations and concluded with final relaxation.

It was summertime and that meant the schedule was more rigorous, with class occurring three times a week instead of two. I loved seeing the difference in my body those summers.

I maintained the headstand until my instructor told us to release the pose. I carefully dropped my legs to the floor, and then happily curled into child's pose. The reality of my life had left my brain, and I was completely absorbed in the present moment. My work was so far away, it might as well have been in another universe. During this time, I worked for a boss who helped me experience firsthand a Culture of Wellbeing. Linda insisted we go home and enjoy full lives outside of work, and my five years of yoga classes were possible because of her determination to let us put ourselves first.

Taking care of our bodies is essential to our wellbeing. Let's talk about four ways we can cherish our physical selves.

1. **Having Fun**

   When we hear the word, "exercise," we think of it as a task or duty that we *should* do. It's a serious and heavy topic, and we're likely magnifying the distance we fall short, as we shame ourselves for not exercising enough. I rarely use this word when talking about my own life. I say instead, "Scout and I walked today and I let her lead the way and she had so much fun that she ran circles around the table when we returned home."

   The Wellness Inventory Certification Training taught me the importance of this fresh perspective—that moving our bodies can be joyful and fun. What did you once enjoy playing as a kid? Whether it was a team sport or pretending you were a mermaid, there were many ways we played that shouldn't be dismissed. What are some ways you can make movement fun as an adult?

As we age, our bodies change, and we may experience more restrictions. Enjoy some self-compassion, and marvel at all that your body *can* still do. Let's focus less on the obligation of "exercise" and instead have fun boosting our physical activity throughout the day.

2. **Stop Sitting and MOVE!**

We sit in front of our computers for much of our workday, then we sit in our cars as we drive home, and then we sit at the kitchen table hunched over our phones, and finally we sprawl in front of the TV, trying to recover from work. Our sedentary behavior, so easy to do in our culture, is being compared to smoking cigarettes in terms of the damage it can cause to our bodies.

When we sit for long periods of time, we increase our chances of heart disease, diabetes, and multiple types of cancer. Research shows that adults in the US are chair-bound for an average of 9.5 hours per day, while the average globally is 4.7 hours per day. We must redesign our lifestyles, as inactivity leads to excess weight, which leads to diseases that cut short our lives.

People who sit for 10 hours or more a day are also more likely to develop dementia, according to a recent study. And here's a big bummer—exercise doesn't undo the risk for dementia after folks have been sedentary that long. Nevertheless, we must continue adding movement to our days.

Here are ways we might unplant our derrieres:

- Tracking your days and understanding how much of your time is sedentary
- Walking during meetings with your coworkers
- Investing in a standing desk—but don't stand so much you experience lower back pain

- Experimenting with a walking pad (a simplified tread-mill that fits under your desk), because any movement is better than remaining slouched in your chair
- Standing and moving around every 90 to 120 minutes, coinciding with your ultradian rhythms, which we discuss further in Chapter 9 – Becoming Your Best at Work
- Walking at lunchtime
- Walking to your coworker's desk, rather than messaging
- Taking the stairs instead of the elevator
- Walking around your home when you're on the phone with your parents

Again, this isn't the time to GO BIG OR GO HOME. It's the time to understand that change is necessary and consider one small step forward. Which of these ideas would be fun for you to try? Start with just one and then add more as your curiosity and desire grow.

3. Counting Our Steps

We've all heard that we're supposed to walk 10,000 steps a day, but is that true? Turns out that 10,000 is more than we need and telling ourselves that we're falling short doesn't help us develop new habits. Men and women who are younger than 60 enjoyed a reduced mortality risk from 8,000 to 10,000 steps each day. Folks older than 60 benefited from 6,000 to 8,000 steps a day.

It's more fun to count steps than to count how many minutes we exercised each week. The US government currently recommends 150 to 300 minutes of moderate aerobic activity. We struggle to translate this into our daily pursuits, and step count may make it into future recommendations. For most folks, 2,000 steps is about one mile.

When I first moved to Colorado, I was unaccustomed to the elevation, and I found myself out of breath after only walking a quarter mile. Over time, we walked further and further, to the delight of our dog. Our lungs eventually adjusted to life at a high altitude, and the daily walks are now extensive. Likewise, if you want to walk more after being inactive, aim for 500 steps a day, which is close to a quarter mile. Every couple of weeks, try walking an additional 500 steps.

While many people love fitness trackers, I personally don't like wearing them. I also don't like carrying my phone with me on walks. My preferences have made it more challenging for me to track my own steps, so I found an affordable, digital counter that clips to my shoes. What works easily for you?

4. **Protecting Ourselves from Forever Chemicals**

I would rather write about the entertaining things Scout did today, but this is an important topic and we have an opportunity to empower ourselves with knowledge. We're unaccustomed to talking about forever chemicals, but it needs to be part of the conversation about our wellbeing both at work and at home.

Humans have created thousands of compounds to help products repel water, grease, and stains. They contain a carbon-fluorine bond; they persist for centuries in nature and while they're formally known as polyfluoroalkyl and perfluoroalkyl substances (PFAS), they've earned the moniker "forever chemicals." These compounds are consistently toxic to our bodies and the environment.

Where might we find a forever chemical? They're laced into items like food packaging, nonstick cookware, stain-resistant carpet and upholstery, paints, waterproof clothing, firefighting foam, solar panels, artificial turf, dental floss, and waterproof cosmetics. These compounds may be useful, but we must ask the question—Is this product absolutely necessary? It's time for consumers to avoid these items and instead purchase the ones that are free of forever chemicals.

So far, scientists have determined that these compounds enter our bodies in three different ways: (1) when we breathe in polluted air, (2) when we eat or drink contaminated food and water, and (3) when we absorb them through our skin.

Almost all Americans have forever chemicals in their blood, according to the Centers for Disease Control and Prevention. You won't be surprised to hear there are links between exposure to forever chemicals and liver damage, kidney disease, cancers, preeclampsia, thyroid disease, and a decreased response to vaccines in children.

> ....
> We have to accept that we can't completely cut out all exposure to forever chemicals, and this makes our activities in all of the 10 Dimensions of Wellbeing even more important.
> ....

State governments have begun banning forever chemicals, and the US Environmental Protection Agency (EPA) updated the drinking water standard to reduce exposure. The EPA also classified two of the forever chemicals as hazardous substances under the Superfund law. As we understand the impact to our health, companies have stopped producing a few of these forever chemicals. These compounds were replaced, however, by new forever chemicals that haven't been studied well.

How can we stay healthy during this time that echoes the Wild West? There are 14,000 known chemicals in food packaging alone, and one-quarter of those have been found by researchers in our blood, breast milk, or hair. We have to accept that we can't completely cut out all exposure to forever chemicals, and this makes our activities in all of the 10 Dimensions of Wellbeing even more important.

There are specific actions that we can take to reduce our exposure, however:

- When possible, buy unpackaged, organic fruits and vegetables.
- Cook at home more often.
- Use PFAS-free cookware, such as ceramic, stainless steel, glass, or cast-iron.
- Avoid microwaving food in takeout and plastic containers.
- If you're using plastic bins to store your food, use larger ones that have less contact with your leftovers.
- When possible, store your leftovers in food-safe glass or ceramic containers. Bring these to restaurants and avoid their to-go containers.
- Store your dog's kibble in food-safe glass or ceramic containers as well.
- Stop buying bottled water.
- Don't reuse plastics meant for single use.
- Wash plastic by hand, not in the dishwasher.
- Avoid microwave popcorn.
- Consider a home water filter that is independently certified to remove specific contaminants.
- Avoid artificial turf and opt for natural materials when landscaping. If you touch the turf, take care to wash your hands with soap and water afterwards.
- Ask yourself if there is a good reason to keep using your waterproof mascara and long-lasting lipstick. Research alternatives and incorporate more PFAS-free cosmetics into your beauty regimen.
- Likewise, seek out rain jackets and snow gear by first checking the brands' websites to see if they offer PFAS-free clothing lines.

PFAS are here to stay, and we must adjust to life with them. It's vital that we learn how to clean them up in the environment, and that we elect leaders who will ban their nonessential use.

···

Tips for Team Leaders

- Consider what physical activity brings you joy and carve out time in your schedule to have fun. Then you can share with your team the meaningful ways you're taking care of your body and encourage them to do the same. Of course, make sure your employees have both a sustainable workload as well as flexibility in their schedules so that they too can enjoy their favorite activities.

- Track your own sedentary hours and make the necessary changes by bringing more light and fun into your life. Help your employees track their hours too and work together to create an environment where they move their bodies more and Zoom less.

- Help your staff understand whether a standing desk and walking pad work in your office culture. Perhaps there are times when it's appropriate, and times it's not, and clarity from you will help them feel successful and valued.

- Instead of sitting at a table, enjoy walking meetings with an employee. Schedule these "Walk & Talks" regularly.

- In the lunchroom, remove plastic cups, dishes, and silverware and replace them with PFAS-free alternatives. Talk with your employees about this change, and help them consider their own decisions at home.

- Whenever possible, purchase furniture and carpeting that is NOT stain-resistant for the office.

••

It's time for us to leave our sedentary ways in the past, and create days filled with joyful movement. It's also time to reduce our exposure to forever chemicals so that we can maintain our health. When we cherish our bodies, we enjoy greater longevity, and there has never been a more crucial time for each of us to focus on our wellbeing.

We can do it!

8

BOOSTING YOUR
MENTAL FITNESS

As I was writing counter-cultural ideas for an article about the wellbeing of fundraisers, my inner critic and judge fretted nonstop in the back of my head, cartwheeling and tumbling to get my attention.

"What is wrong with you? You can't say that!" my judge cautioned me.

I was in my home office, surrounded by piles of books and papers, slowly pecking at my keyboard. My brows furrowed in concentration as I explored fresh ideas, and until the rude interruption, I had enjoyed working in a state of flow.

In my article, I described the impossible choice fundraisers face. They can take care of themselves with healthy boundaries between work and home, or they can work longer hours to raise more money and avoid layoffs. I wrote that fundraisers need to take care of themselves first, before their job responsibilities. I also wrote that self-care needs to be part of a fundraiser's job description, as well as an important piece of their code of ethics.

Folks in the nonprofit world don't say these things out loud. As we've discussed in earlier chapters, there's a myth in our society that employees who burn out are weak, but actually it's the most committed and dedicated people who become overwhelmed and fatigued.

I had recently begun my coach training with Positive Intelligence® (PQ). It's an exciting, science-based program that helps you understand and identify your mean-spirited inner voices. Recognizing the tenor of your own judge was an important piece of this work, and I hadn't heard much from mine yet. We all have this critic who is quick to judge ourselves and others.

Shirzad Chamine, author of the book *Positive Intelligence* and creator of the coach-training program, openly shared how his inner judge was loud and vicious. He referred to his judge as an "executioner." In comparison, my judge was wily and quiet, waiting for the right moment to pounce.

I stopped typing and considered what my judge wanted me to do— *stop writing provocative things. NOW.* I have heard this message before.

Then I heard my judge sneer, "Who are you to say these things? You're getting too big for your britches."

> We tell ourselves that we need our inner voices to be hurtful so that we maintain our record of high achievement. Yet the opposite is true!

Every time my judge has told me to stop writing, I know I'm about to say something meaningful and important. *Every time.* So I kept writing. I also marveled at the comment about my britches, and decided to name my judge "Mr. Britches." While his name was charming, I understood that my judge didn't want me to play big in life. He was deadly serious.

I was delighted when *Advancing Philanthropy*, a magazine for fundraisers, published my article, despite the attempts of devious Mr. Britches to sabotage my efforts.

We all have voices in our heads. Sometimes the voice is compassionate and loving, but often, the words are so unkind that we would never talk that way to our friends. Unfortunately, we all have our own version of

Mr. Britches, and these voices come from a place of fear. They regularly remind us:

You're not good enough.
They're going to discover that you don't know what you're doing.
You should have kept your mouth shut in that meeting.
You're weak and lazy for falling behind again.
You used to be so motivated and driven—what has happened?

Sound familiar? We tell ourselves that we need our inner voices to be hurtful so that we maintain our record of high achievement.

Yet the opposite is true!

You may be surprised to learn that these voices (which are really saboteurs, not our friends) *decrease* our productivity by creating additional stress and fatigue that can lead to burnout. We experience self-doubt, anxiety, and unhappiness, and ultimately we learn that criticizing ourselves offers only the illusion of control.

The Formula for Greater Mental Fitness

When we're mentally fit, instead of staying upset, we enjoy the ability to handle the trials of life with a positive mindset. This sounds great, but how do we get there?

It's not easy, especially considering we've created neural pathways over decades that we default to when we're stressed. Here's the great news—research shows that we *can* create new neural pathways! There is always hope for change.

Our brains have "plasticity," a quality that allows them to be adaptable to new experiences. We can rewire our neural pathways so that we respond to challenging situations in a new way. Rather than reacting from the part of the brain that's motivated through fear, anger, and guilt, we can learn to shift our thinking to a region focused on empathy, creativity, and purpose.

There are three key steps to boosting our mental fitness:

1.   Intercepting your judge and saboteurs when they act up
2.   Leaving worry behind and experiencing the present moment
3.   Shifting to a positive mindset

I appreciate the succinctness of these ideas, but they're not a quick fix. Becoming more mentally fit is a lifelong journey.

1.   **Intercepting Your Judge and Saboteurs**
     Shirzad Chamine completed factor analysis research and determined that we have nine specific saboteurs and one judge that we need to be wary of. Examples of saboteurs include the Hyper-Achiever, the Controller, the Stickler, etc. You can learn to intercept them and prevent them from damaging your mindset.

     These critical voices originate from fear and promise that you'll be happier if you accomplish more, control your surroundings, and create perfect order. When you've achieved this, you'll find your saboteurs have moved the goal line!

     We likely were born with amazing strengths that we relied on throughout the challenges of our childhood, and over time, we overused these strengths, creating mental habits for our feelings and thoughts. These automatic habits morph into saboteurs by the time we're adults. Our saboteurs represent extra baggage that we unwittingly carry, and they're not part of our authentic selves.

     If you want to learn more about yourself, you can take a free Saboteur Assessment at their website (PositiveIntelligence. com). While I am a Certified Positive Intelligence Coach™, I don't get paid when you do this. (Also, I'd like to share—I'm an independent member of the PQ Coach program, and not an employee, agent, or representative of Positive Intelligence LLC. In addition, my coaching program is independently owned and operated by me, and is not affiliated with or endorsed by Positive Intelligence LLC. Just in case you were wondering!)

When I speak publicly about mental fitness, I share these three tips for taking the assessment:

i.   Remember that everyone has saboteurs, and there is no shame here. There is NOT a specific saboteur that is more desirable than others, as they're all equally destructive.

ii. When you see your assessment results, ask yourself which of the saboteurs you are most motivated to pursue. Just focus on one, and as you weaken it, the others will be affected.

iii. The absolute scores don't matter, so don't worry that something is "too high." What does matter are your relative scores. What are your three highest saboteurs? This is meaningful information.

How can we recognize that we're stuck in a place of fear?

Multiple outstanding coach-training programs helped me understand that it's common for us to spend our days going back and forth from love to fear. Often, however, we're unaware of our shifts and we become stuck in fear. When we begin to register our internal processes, we can pay closer attention.

My clients share that when their saboteurs get the best of them, they experience it in their bodies. They may feel the stress in their tight necks and shoulders, or notice that they're hunched over from the heaviness. Some feel their stomachs churning, while others take shorter breaths as their chests constrict. Their emotions may range from disquiet to dread, and all of them have an unkind, inner voice measuring their worth. "Your achievements to date aren't particularly impressive." *Ouch.*

Pay attention to your own experience with your saboteurs. What is true for you?

Ask yourself these questions:

- Where in your body do you experience fear?
- What emotions do you feel when your inner critic evaluates you?
- What lies are your saboteurs telling you?

It takes courage to pay attention to your fears and understand their impact on you. Kudos! These questions help you understand how our thoughts and emotions are tied together.

I have enjoyed some good pity parties for myself in the past. You may be thinking that it feels good to wallow in your own unhappy feelings too. Can wallowing be good for us?

One of my favorite images from this training is of a hand on a hot stove. This is a great reminder that pain is helpful in the smallest of doses. When our hand is on a hot stove, our pain response tells us to immediately move our hand to prevent a serious injury. Likewise, our negative emotions are useful as a quick alert so that we can make necessary changes. When you continue to wallow and stay upset, your brain is locked in a place without access to creativity and resourcefulness, so it's important to intercept your saboteurs as quickly as possible. While staying in your negative emotions may feed a dark part of yourself, it ultimately makes it harder to respond well.

It's important that we discredit our saboteurs and take away their power, and this is the opposite of wallowing.

Have lots of compassion for yourself, as discovering more about your saboteurs is challenging. They may even become more vocal and mean as you focus instead on a positive mindset.

2. **Experiencing the Present Moment**

Our saboteurs want us to keep spinning along the same unhappy neural pathways. It takes focus, practice, and patience to stop reacting as usual, and instead take a moment to switch gears.

When you step away from your fears and experience the present moment, you command your mind to create new neural pathways, allowing you to shift from your biggest worries to your greatest hopes.

When we focus our attention on physical sensations, we find ourselves in the present moment. Just like building muscles at the gym, we can build our muscles of mental fitness with repetitions. There are many interesting ways to do these reps, and you may prefer to think of them as a meditative push-up or breathing exercise. However you personally understand it, these repetitions can be as short as 10 seconds!

I loved my yoga classes and was taught to formally meditate after stretching, so my body was flexible and I could sit cross-legged comfortably, on the floor with a small cushion. I was taught to close my eyes, wear the same clothes, sit in the same place in my home, and ideally face east. I was also taught to use incense as a reminder for my body to leave daily life behind and more quickly return to meditative states. This was useful information, and it helped me to become quite the yoga enthusiast, at the time.

Now I especially love that we can do these reps with our eyes open, in the middle of a tough meeting at work. We can feel calm and clearheaded during our busy days, and not just when we're meditating at home.

What might it look like to focus on the present moment? Here are some examples:

- Seeing – Look at one thing in front of you. What colors do you notice? What shapes?

- Touching – Hold something in your hand and gently feel the textures. What do you notice about the temperature?

- Hearing – Wherever you are, pay attention to the sound that is furthest away. Now focus on the sound that is closest.

- Sensing Your Body – Feel the weight of your body on your chair. Notice your feet resting on the floor. Have fun wiggling your toes!

- Breathing – Pay attention as you gently inhale and exhale. For a longer repetition, inhale to the count of four and exhale to the count of eight. Do this several times.

Have fun experimenting with these different repetitions to see which you most enjoy. Discover which you can comfortably do with your eyes open. Also, which one do you like best with your eyes closed? There's no right or wrong.

I personally enjoy using a small rock to help me build my mental-fitness muscles. I admire its beauty and notice the swirl of colors. I also pay attention to its texture. I love rocks, and using them during the day is a quick path to gratitude, as I think about Mother Nature making these beauties and the joy they bring me.

After switching from fear and focusing on the present moment, some of my clients appreciate a quick prayer. Whether you have a relationship with God, Lakshmi, Allah, the Buddha, or the Universe and the Goddess, invoking them to help you come from a place of love rather than fear can make a difference. We'll talk more about that in Chapter 13 – Creating an Inspired Life.

3. **Shifting to a Positive Mindset**

Once you have stopped worrying and instead focused on the physical sensations of the present moment, it's time to embrace a positive mindset. Shirzad discusses more than just a mindset—he describes our natural, authentic essence. While our saboteurs are unwelcome hitchhikers, our true selves are beautiful and unchanging. He refers to this essence as our "sage."

Our saboteurs and sage live in different regions of the brain. The fear-based voices come from parts of the left brain, while our sage superpowers live in parts of the right brain. Our saboteurs motivate us through negative emotions—such as fear, shame, guilt, anger, and insecurity—while the sage motivates not from fear but love, and we experience empathy, curiosity, creativity, joy, and purpose.

Earlier, you considered how you experienced saboteurs in your body and mind. Notice now your experience in love. Your body surely feels different, perhaps lighter and more expansive. Maybe you're less hunched and standing up straighter. Your emotions are now positive, and your inner voice is one of self-acceptance and wisdom.

When we have a positive mindset and come from love, all the dimensions of our lives benefit. Everything is interconnected, and when we boost one area of our lives, the others improve as well. We sleep better, feel reverence in nature, and use social media as a force for good.

Our mindset even impacts how our bodies respond to vaccines, according to research. Folks with positive mindsets about the COVID-19 vaccine experienced less stress the day of the injection. They had fewer side effects, and some had higher antibodies six months later. Wow! I get excited when science proves what we intuitively know—that our brains and bodies are deeply interconnected, even boosting our immune systems.

It's easier for us to intellectually understand the benefits of a positive mindset than it is to experience it and make healthy choices for ourselves in the moment.

How can you make better choices in the moment?

When our harsh inner voices tell us that a situation is BAD, we judge it and postpone possible happiness until the situation has changed. What if the situation had a silver lining? We can find a gift or opportunity, even when it's hard, even when we have to create that gift ourselves. This "sage perspective" makes our days less scary, as we understand that when events turn upside down, we can learn from them and use valuable lessons to create better lives.

We have a critical choice to make when tough things happen. We can follow our old neural circuitry and experience a vicious reaction of our saboteurs. Or we can see the event as a gift and instead enjoy a reaction of our positive mindset and sage. Whichever happens is based on the perspective you bring (This is BAD vs. This is a GIFT).

Likewise, Kate Sweeny, a psychology professor at the University of California at Riverside, describes the best strategy for managing uncertainty, based on her research. When we worry about an unknown outcome, we experience negative and repetitive thoughts that poison our wellbeing, resulting in poor sleep and a weakened immune system.

She recommends that, instead of worrying, we boost our optimism (by distracting ourselves with our favorite activities and enjoying a state of flow) for as long as possible. Then, *for just a few minutes*, we should practice "predemption," a technique where we consider at least one positive thing that could come from the worst outcome. Again, notice where you feel it in your body. If the worst does happen, predemption is an effective way to absorb the setback, feel less distraught, and keep fighting for change.

Whether we call it the sage perspective or predemption, finding the gift in a challenging situation serves us well.

The Impact of our Mindset on Burnout

Before we began working together, my client, Gina, experienced burnout. She didn't see any gifts from this distressing time. Her inner voices regularly told her that she was deeply flawed for finally buckling under the workload she previously had endured:

There's something wrong with you.
You're imperfect. Flawed. Unprofessional.
You don't belong here.
People want you to take charge already.
Your worth is based on what your team accomplishes.

With these voices assessing her performance and supposedly guiding her, she spiraled down into self-doubt and melancholy.

As we talked about in Chapter 2 – Tallying the Costs of Burnout, the World Health Organization identified three symptoms of burnout: exhaustion, cynicism, and ineffectiveness. Before we worked together, Gina's mindset impacted all of these.

As Gina believed the lies of her saboteurs, she worked even harder to prove them wrong. She doubled her efforts to control her team, while also frantically working to hide her "inadequacy" and disparaging herself for not being perfect. Gina **exhausted** her body and spirit.

Her inner judge told her that she couldn't be happy in the present moment of struggle. Happiness and fulfillment became elusive in all areas of her life. She also questioned if she fit in with the other managers, and she became **cynical** and distrustful.

Ultimately, after years of overwork, Gina found her creativity shriveled, her decision-making clouded, and her efficiency in the toilet. At this point, she realized if she didn't make drastic changes, she would no longer produce her best work. Gina felt all but **ineffective**, for the first time in her career.

Recognizing she was desperate to feel good again, she reached out. With coaching, she understood how her saboteurs led her repeatedly to feel insecure and controlling, and as she learned to let go, she discovered the relief of trusting her team. They began to thrive with greater autonomy.

Likewise, I accelerated my own journey to burnout by listening to the lies of my saboteurs. This doesn't have to be our destiny, however. You can choose to find a gift in the overwhelm, and take steps toward greater health and wellbeing, rather than toward fatigue, burnout, and disease.

As my body and spirit slowly recovered, I realized I wanted to understand burnout on all levels. What could I have done differently, as an individual, and what leadership issues were at play? I knew I liked working with people one on one, based on my time as a major gifts officer, and I believed I'd make a great coach. While I didn't have the vocabulary yet, I was applying the wisdom of the sage perspective and finding the gift in my burnout. In my coaching classes, I healed and saved myself. I also set my course to save others lost on the same destructive path.

I wish I could have told myself to find a gift in my last years as a fundraiser. Rather than beating myself up, I would have enjoyed self-compassion. I also would have reframed the tough times at work as learning opportunities for my next career.

I use my training, research, and personal experience to help my clients in a way that I couldn't help myself during my own trials. This is what I share with my clients, when they're struggling at work:

You have an amazing opportunity now. You're empowered to do what's best for you, and you don't have to make that decision today. Until then, you can use each challenging event that happens at your work as a stepping stone for a job that is

better aligned with your values. You deserve the most fulfilling career. When the leadership is untrustworthy, you can consider how you want to one day lead your own team. When you're overworked, you can learn more about creating a Culture of Wellbeing, if not now, then at a future organization. You can turn every tough experience into a gift for your future self.

At one point, I thought burnout was the most painful experience of my career and I wished it had never happened. Now, however, I'm grateful. Without my burnout, I would not have been inspired to discover my career as a coach, author, and speaker.

Furthermore, when we do all we can to take care of ourselves, and we find that we're still burning out, then we need to accept that there are strategic management issues. It's time to find an organization that cultivates a Culture of Wellbeing, rather than overwork. You deserve it!

Tips for Team Leaders

- Every organization has a culture, and this culture usually reflects the saboteurs of the top leaders. Did you catch that? *Your organization's culture reflects the saboteurs of your top leaders.* How has this impacted your team?

- If you want to introduce mental-fitness concepts to your team, begin by understanding your own saboteurs. Help your staff understand that you struggle with your own voices. This vulnerability and courage will build trust and open them to the idea of discovering more about their own inner critics.

- Hire a professional coach, trained in mental fitness, to transform you and your team. Choose a certified coach who understands the challenges of burnout and offers evidence-based programs to fast-track your organization back to a Culture of Wellbeing.

- Remember the two primal forces (fear and love) and learn to recognize how you're experiencing them in your body, emotions, and thoughts. Relate to your staff, as much as possible, coming from love.

••

Addressing your inner critic takes courage and dedication, so recognize your small steps forward. When we boost our mental fitness, it's not a one-time sprint, but a promise to ourselves that each day, for the rest of our lives, we'll try to find the gift in the hardest situations. It's a marathon of self-love!

We can do it!

9

BECOMING YOUR BEST AT WORK

Long before I became a coach, I had the opportunity to work with Linda, and to discover what it was like to feel cherished as an employee. During the first week on my job, I worked late a couple of evenings, to demonstrate I was a responsible, hard-working employee. Linda's response?

With her purple reading glasses perched in her spiky, white hair, she said evenly, *"Your overtime doesn't impress me. Go home and take care of yourself."* Wow!

Also during my first week, in Linda's absence, I worked with volunteers who were snail-mailing our monthly newsletter. After introducing myself and helping them get organized, I read for the first time the freshly printed issue and immediately saw that we had misspelled the name of our own organization on the front page. *Ugh.* While a coworker and the volunteers wanted to stay on schedule and mail the newsletter as it was, I disagreed. Without understanding what Linda would do in my situation, I went by my own instincts and halted the mailing of the newsletter.

I anxiously awaited Linda's return to the office. I was concerned she'd be upset with me for blowing her timeline, but instead she responded with gratitude for my attention to detail and willingness to make things right for our donors. *Whew!*

I didn't understand fully at the time, but during that first week, Linda demonstrated over and over the power of a Culture of Wellbeing. She promoted healthy boundaries between work and home, while also giving me autonomy to make hard decisions that benefited our team in the long run.

Under Linda's guidance, I enjoyed many opportunities for growth. At every annual review, she offered me a raise. She also thought ahead about the different roles I could play in the department, allowing me to learn and to develop my skills and strengths.

While she encouraged me to grow and meet my fundraising goals, she also understood my love of travel and adventure. When I asked her if I could save my vacation days and take a six-week vacation through the Southwest, she agreed. And when I returned early because my marriage fell apart in Colorado, she listened to my sadness.

In the future, I would experience the opposite of this warm and welcoming culture. I would feel isolated and gravely misunderstood. I remember how, the one time I ever said NO to my boss, Michelle (I had told her calmly that I didn't have time to take on an additional assignment that night), she frowned unhappily. I wish that we had talked about how I couldn't fit in one more task while also managing a capital campaign, but we didn't. We also should have figured things out during the flow of work, but that never happened either. Instead, she waited for months and then used it as a reason to deny my raise during my annual review.

I didn't understand yet that the tough times at work can catalyze great change and inspire our future careers. This reframe helps us feel motivated and aligned with our biggest life goals, even when our current jobs are difficult. While I didn't understand how to be my best at work, I pursued this subject passionately when I returned to school to become a coach who helps dedicated leaders who are burning out. I remembered the importance of healthy boundaries between work and home; in addition, we must have the autonomy to say NO.

Establishing Healthy Boundaries Between Work and Home

Whether we work from home or in an office, there are four key elements to building better boundaries between our work and our home.

1. **Creating Daily Routines**

   I encourage you to create routines each day. For example, shower and change into fresh clothes for work. Whether you're working at home or in an office, sit in an area designed for focusing your efforts.

   Set a time to begin and end your workday that doesn't require much overtime. Then, at the end of your day, sign off your computer and step away. Give yourself and your employees permission to turn off the notifications on their phones after hours. Just because you're a team leader, your salary is at a certain level, you don't have kids, or you have nowhere else to go—this doesn't mean you must be available and working from early in the morning until midnight. Whatever our situation, we deserve downtime.

2. **Refraining from After-Hours Contact**

   We need time away from work to recuperate. When we return to work after rejuvenating, we feel more resilient and creative, and we're better problem-solvers. When our time away from work (in the evenings, on the weekends, or on vacations) is interrupted by emails and texts from our colleagues, we don't renew ourselves as well.

   Do you struggle when you receive an email in the evening, wondering if you should respond? It's important that all members of the team talk openly about expectations of being available after hours. Furthermore, leaders must model healthy boundaries themselves.

3. **Taking Rejuvenating Breaks Every 90 to 120 Minutes**

Similar to our phases when we sleep, we have cycles throughout the day as we naturally move from high energy to low energy, multiple times a day. These 90- to 120-minute cycles are called "ultradian rhythms" and toward the end of each, our bodies crave recovery. When this happens, we might feel hungry, yawn, or want to walk around because we've lost our focus.

Unfortunately, we're conditioned to stay at our desks and plow through our task list rather than listen to the needs of our bodies. (After all, ideal employees are tough and don't need pee breaks.) What reservoir of energy we may have is more quickly depleted if we don't renew ourselves.

How can you take care of yourself throughout the day? By completely disengaging from work at the end of these cycles. You can do the following:

- Go for a walk outside
- Talk with a coworker in the breakroom (about something besides work)
- Listen to music
- Take deep breaths
- Enjoy a 20-minute power nap
- Meditate
- Walk up and down the stairs
- Enjoy any healthy ritual that helps you to change your focus from work

The quality of your renewal break is more important than its length, so have fun finding your own personal ways to disengage. Which are you most excited to try?

Remember that stepping away from your desk doesn't mean that you're unprofessional. It means that your body and mind will function better throughout the day if you renew your energy.

By taking care of yourself, you'll feel better, which is the most important outcome. You'll also be more creative and productive.

4. **Enjoying Guilt-Free Vacations**

    Think about your favorite vacation. If you travelled, where did you go? You had the chance to explore and learn, and each day likely brought something unfamiliar, providing you with a sense of adventure. The beautiful landscapes and scenery connected you to something greater. Whether we're hiking the Camino de Santiago or ambling through a Redwood grove, our steps are sacred.

    As you reflect on your favorite vacation, who travelled with you? Often, we choose to travel with our chosen inner circle. It will be these memories that we cherish and that give our life meaning and fulfillment. I'm 99 percent sure that working overtime at your office will NOT be what you are most grateful for at the end of your life.

    Furthermore, we recharge our depleted energy when we travel. We're not robots, we're humans, and we need to step away from the frantic pace of our endless to-do list. We need to renew. Vacations are good for our bodies, minds, and spirits, which is our most important goal, as we inherently deserve to feel good. It's also true that we'll return to work happier, more creative, and more efficient.

    I've heard folks talk about how incredible it would be to have *unlimited vacation* time. Sounds amazing, doesn't it? You could finally take that trip to Patagonia. In reality, however, companies like Netflix and social media platforms discovered that their employees actually take even fewer vacation days when they have unlimited time off. The companies develop a "warrior mentality," which is the opposite of a Culture of Wellbeing. They see taking time off as a weakness, and peer pressure keeps the employees stuck in their office, rather than Argentina.

    Definitely NOT my idea of a guilt-free vacation!

If unlimited vacation time isn't the key, what is? A fascinating experiment by Neil Pasricha and Shashank Nigam shows that one solution may be **Mandatory Vacations**. That's right, my friend, with this model, everyone absolutely positively must take a scheduled vacation multiple times a year. Each vacation is scheduled well in advance, and every person goes. There are no snide remarks or raised eyebrows, because there is finally no guilt for taking time away from the office. YES!

Employees in the experiment returned feeling happier and more fulfilled, as many had checked off items from their bucket list. This sounds downright *dreamy* to me.

And while you are vacationing, remember that it's important to leave your laptop at home. Create healthy boundaries and fully enjoy your time away! Give yourself permission to completely disconnect, because you deserve this. You'll also return feeling better rested and rejuvenated.

Saying NO at Work

As we discussed in Chapter 2 – Tallying the Costs of Burnout, one of our three basic psychological needs is autonomy. When good leaders empower us to make decisions on our own about projects at work, we feel engaged and motivated. When bad managers micromanage our efforts, we lack autonomy and don't have control over our workloads. We become exhausted and weary.

According to Dr. Amy Arnsten at Yale School of Medicine, burnout thins the grey matter in our prefrontal cortex, making us more likely to make mistakes. It also enlarges the amygdala, which means we're more likely to see the world as dangerous. If we believe we're in charge of our daily tasks at work, then these brain changes don't happen. It is when we lack autonomy and can't control the stressor that the damage from burnout occurs.

I'm curious to find out if we also have these same brain changes when we can't control the stressor at home (hello single moms and caregivers!). Our autonomy is key to our ability to say NO. We need to be empowered to say NO, even when our job descriptions include "additional duties as assigned," because some managers are unable to put your own wellbeing first. You must do this yourself.

....

It is when we lack autonomy and can't control the stressor that the damage from burnout occurs.

....

As we talked about in Chapter 8 – Boosting Your Mental Fitness, we all have a callous inner critic in our heads that lies to us and creates anxiety. Saying NO is challenging for many people, especially folks whose voices want them to be people pleasers or avoiders. Furthermore, when managers are controlling, there is little room for discussion, and the employees quickly learn to complete the tasks the way their manager demands. There's no room for creative problem-solving or getting it right the second time in these cultures.

We're not taught how to say NO at work, and we haven't seen it successfully modeled by our bosses or teammates. What we do see is people acquiescing to the demands on their time outside of the office, and then the unspoken pressure that we are supposed to work extra hours as well, for the privilege of being part of the team. This is a path to burnout, and it's bonkers.

Before you can effectively say NO at work, you must know what first to welcome into your life. What must you say YES to, for ultimate fulfillment and joy? If you're not sure where to begin, no worries. Each of the 10 Dimensions of Wellbeing that I'm sharing in this book could be a meaningful starting point. Which one most resonates with you? Start from that specific dimension and notice how, when you improve yourself in one area, all the others benefit too. Since your *Work Comes Third*, it will be easier to say NO when you better understand your greatest priorities.

What should we say NO to?

- Unmanageable workloads
- Lack of control over our assignments
- Unreasonable time pressure
- Unfair and disrespectful treatment
- Unwanted sexual advances
- Ambiguous communication about our goals
- Inequitable compensation
- Lack of support from our managers

This is not a complete list. What unhelpful behaviors at work would you like to say NO to?

Let me share advice about the logistics of how to say NO (and the book, *Nonviolent Communication* by Marshall B. Rosenberg, PhD, offers valuable pointers). For starters, talk about yourself and not the other person. You'll know you're successful with this when you use the word "I" frequently. Next, think through how you feel about a certain situation. What emotions come up for you? Then recognize what needs you have that are unmet. Finally, consider how you'd like to work together to create change.

When I was burning out, I didn't share with my boss my feelings or needs. See below for things I wish I had said. I encourage you to try on each statement and decide how it fits. Understand what is true for you and use it to jumpstart a conversation of your own.

- "When you assigned me additional responsibilities, I felt stressed and overwhelmed. I need more help prioritizing, because I can't juggle all these tasks. I'm hoping we can figure this out together."

- "I'm a single woman with many responsibilities outside of work. I want you to understand that I don't have a partner helping at home. I need more flexibility in my schedule."

- "I have creative passions that are drying up because of my workload. This worries me, because I have quite the artistic side and I need it to flourish. I want to talk with you about maintaining healthy boundaries between work and home. I need the weekends to myself."

- "The workload and job responsibilities are unsustainable. This is not a reflection of my worth. This is a leadership issue."

- "I am fried on all levels after completing this capital campaign. I need an eight-week sabbatical to see if I can rejuvenate."

- "I don't feel like I fit in with the team. I don't feel safe sharing my authentic self here. I have experienced before the joy of being the heart of the team, and feeling like an outsider now is tough for me. Please help."

- "I feel like I'm burning out. I want you to know that it's the most passionate and dedicated employees who burn out, not the weakest."

Whew.

If you can share your needs in a healthy way, it will give your boss the opportunity to respond. It's possible she will listen and help you, and this can become a series of conversations that build trust. It's also possible that she won't help you, so remember that you don't have control over her response. What is success for you in this conversation? Calmly sharing your needs, regardless of how she reacts. I hope you will recognize the courage it takes to be vulnerable and authentic, especially at work.

I discovered that I was replaceable at my last fundraising job, and if you discover that as well, make career decisions based on your inherent worth, not on how someone treats you.

Tips for Team Leaders

- Remember that burnout is about more than the number of hours your staff work; it's also about how they're supervised. Your behavior impacts how your employees experience their workload. When you're reactive and judgmental, they feel misunderstood. When you're reflective and empathetic, your staff members feel more inspired and supported in their work, and they're less stressed and frazzled.

- Focus less on how or when your employees complete their responsibilities and focus more on outcomes. Give them the freedom to enjoy their own style and preferences at work.

- Respect the needs of your team to rejuvenate at home, and do NOT email or text them after hours or on vacation. Focus on planning ahead and developing contingency plans. Healthy boundaries are important to create a Culture of Wellbeing!

- Lead by example, by taking vacations and leaving your work in the office. Also, be sure you take breaks to renew your energy throughout your workdays. Your employees will follow your precedent.

- Enlist your dedicated HR professionals to walk the floor at 5:00 p.m. and encourage staff to go home!

- Promote mandatory vacations at your organization. Create a culture of delegation and shared responsibility, so that each employee can leave for vacation knowing others will help cover her tasks. Consider telling your employees that their vacation days are paid only if they don't contact the office!

- Provide a tranquil space in the office where employees can rest and recharge—but don't create expectations that your staff should sleep there overnight. When *Work Comes Third*, going home to our favorite people is a top priority.

- Banish any warrior mentality and peer pressure that discourages employees from taking time off. Create a culture that instead honors the needs of your employees to rejuvenate.

- Build a foundation of trust and autonomy with your employees so that they feel safe saying NO. If you have concerns, provide feedback immediately during the flow of work, and don't retaliate later.

- A Culture of Wellbeing provides safety and acceptance for employees to speak up. You play a big role in fostering this culture by rewarding people who share how they feel, even when it's negative. Allowing your employees to share their truths ultimately creates a team that is more innovative and engaged.

••

Imagine the relief everyone will feel when we respect the healthy boundaries between work and home. Leaders and employees alike will recuperate better. They'll also enjoy a sense of adventure on their trips and create memories that last a lifetime. In addition, when employees rejuvenate away from the office, they return to work feeling more creative and effective. When we give all employees the autonomy they require to oversee their daily tasks at work (including allowing them to say NO) we create a Culture of Wellbeing where people thrive.

We can do it!

10

INDULGING YOUR CREATIVE PASSIONS

Finally, I was allowed into the secret room. I had waited for weeks to discover what mysteries hid behind the door. At the appointed time, I entered the room, carrying my camera and a bag of my most beautiful glass insulators, and my photography instructor cheerily greeted me inside.

We were in the studio, a coveted spot at the community college where each Saturday morning I had sharpened my skills and appreciated the creativity of my fellow students. While we usually met in the classroom, we were invited one by one to use the studio on this special day, and I was so excited I had fidgeted in my seat.

Most of my fellow photographers brought friends or family to pose as their subjects, allowing the students to practice their skills in the studio. I did not bring a person. I love taking shots of forgotten spaces, so when people find their way into my photographs, I feel like something has gone intolerably awry. On that Saturday, I brought my glass insulators to photograph in the studio. These are antiques that once adorned the tops of telegraph and telephone poles, helping people communicate in the early 1900s. They come in many shapes and colors, and I discovered one style (CD 154) that reminded me of a gorgeous candy jar. I had collected a few and I couldn't wait to see how they'd glow under the lights.

I placed the insulators on a white table, and with my instructor's help, changed the backdrop and adjusted the lights. Initially, I took shots of the insulators individually, but it was when I gathered them together in a riot of colorful glass that I lost myself in joy, which often happens when I play with my camera. The photos I took that day are still some of my favorites.

I loved everything about those Saturday classes. They were challenging without feeling overwhelming. While at times I worried about my Photoshop skills, I savored the new tools and techniques I learned to improve my craft.

When I left the classroom, I couldn't wait to get home to see my photos, big and beautiful, on my computer screen. As I loaded up my car with my camera bag and insulators, my chest tightened, and I felt sad that the class was over. Then as I drove home, I couldn't listen to my favorite music because I felt distressed that the best part of my weekend was over, and of course, that work was looming on Monday.

Monday morning was still days away, and I was already dreading it. I learned to numb my feelings of discontent and unhappiness so that I could cope with another stressful week. I didn't know it then, but every time I dulled my emotions, I marched myself on the continuum of well-being toward chronic stress, burnout, and disease.

I love photography and writing, and as I spiraled into burnout, I participated in multiple classes and workshops, visited art museums, and enjoyed my vacations with my dog, Boo. My camera was my constant companion. Despite my attempts to indulge in my creative passions, over time my energy waned and eventually I had nothing to give beyond work. As my aspirations for my favorite pursuits fizzled in this new reality, I finally heard my internal alarm bells clanging furiously.

Everything Creative Is Play

After I burned out and quit my job, you won't be surprised to hear that I immersed myself in my photography and writing. In hindsight, I can see how that helped me to recover. These creative activities saved me. They healed my spirit.

What are your passions? Keep in mind that everything creative is play. In a Culture of Wellbeing, work no longer comes first. In my Wellness Inventory Certification Training, the coaches discussed how, in our society, we're obsessed with work deadlines and we forget how to have fun, but the truth is that playing recharges us and is life-giving.

Here are some ideas of favorite pastimes: gardening, hiking, sports, board games, cooking, beekeeping, loving on your pet, laughing with friends, playing with kids, crafts, decorating, karting (go-kart racing), meditation, reading, massage, rockhounding, and daydreaming. And of course, photography! Each person loves different activities, and what is drudgery for one is play for another, so it's important to understand what energizes you.

My clients succeed when they schedule their favorite activities first. What does this mean? They make play their first priority and schedule work around their creative activities, vacations, and time with their spouses.

Embracing a Beginner's Mindset

In *Be Bad First*, author Erika Andersen encourages us to prepare for the unknown future by learning to be comfortable with being a novice. Every day.

Our favorite pastimes help us become better learners, and the tumultuous, ever-changing 21st century that we find ourselves in demands we embrace the mindset of a beginner. Our amount of shared knowledge, thanks to the internet, is skyrocketing. Technology advances hourly. We're living in one of the most amazing times in history!

We're also living in a troubling time, as it's in our nature to relish being experts at our jobs, yet in this new environment, we must be novices again and again. We are now in a world where best practices are constantly changing. We must learn new things that may not fit with our old ideas.

Who wants to be a newbie, when being a master is so much more pleasing to our egos? You want to be good at your job and to progress from novice to expert as smoothly and quickly as possible.

Hobbies, such as photography, karting, and cooking, are fantastic ways to get in touch with the part of us that doesn't completely wig out over being a rookie. Being a white belt can be a fun change of perspective after always having to be an expert at work. We can pay attention to our behavior while enjoying our favorite activities, and then respond to learning opportunities at work in similar ways.

> There is a joy in the exploration, and a lightheartedness in not having to have all the answers.

I remember shooting photos of two friends karting at a local racetrack. As rookies, they were both still learning how to maintain their karts, as well as how to drive competitively. They were curious, inquisitive, and quick to learn new skills.

I showed up, camera in hand, determined to learn how to capture speed. I wanted to know how to shoot photos that had a blurry background, but the karts were in focus, and I was willing to take shots that involved actual people for this learning opportunity. I was eager to practice panning my camera, moving it at the same speed as the action.

That morning, I considered success to be one good photo taken by panning. Just one. Success for my friends was learning more about driving. And to not break any bones. **Our success was about satisfying our curiosity** and none of us minded that we were still learning. There is a joy in the exploration, and a lightheartedness in not having to have all the answers.

What is your favorite hobby? What do you most enjoy about it? Do you feel a sense of childlike wonder when you're fully participating in it?

You can use this same sense of wonder, this curiosity, when you're at work. Catch yourself thinking, "I wonder . . ." or "What if . . .?" and then follow your curiosity to fresh ideas. Embracing your curiosity at work with a novice frame of mind makes you more open to learning something new.

Also, when we're enjoying our favorite pastimes, it's easier to **allow ourselves to screw up**. My karting friends have endured their share of rookie mistakes on the track. One of them forgot to bolt down the brake, making it impossible to stop. Another forgot to bolt down the accelerator. They frequently have sore chests from their escapades on the track, and one returned home with broken ribs.

As for me and my photography, I have made lots of mistakes too. I returned from shooting pictures of baby owls to discover that I never put the memory card in my camera. Another time, I left behind my camera at a national monument, and it was gone when I returned. *Poof!* The biggest WTF moment was when a horse chomped down on my right hand when we were on a photo tour of Iceland. On that trip, I visited the doctor, and I also learned a new skill—how to take photos with my left hand. I love every one of my shaky pictures from that tour, as they are reminders of my willingness to adapt and again wear my white belt.

What newbie mistakes have you made while enjoying your hobby? How easily are you able to smile about it? Your willingness to be a novice, to learn new things even though it means you're going to screw up, will serve you well at work.

Flow—I Love That for You!

When we're in a state of flow (coined by Mihaly Csikszentmihalyi) we enjoy being completely immersed in a task. We forget the outside world and focus intently on our activity. We feel energized, creative, and productive as we lose track of time.

One of my clients loves to paint, and when she's holding her brush, she easily slips into the zone. She shared that this is one of the best feelings she has experienced. It's exciting that under certain conditions, *anyone* can enjoy this state, as it's universal.

As we experience flow, our prefrontal cortex, responsible for planning and decision-making, becomes less active. Our brains release chemicals, including dopamine and endorphins, allowing us to completely engage in our tasks. As a result, we experience heightened creativity as our thinking becomes less inhibited and we spontaneously free-associate to generate new ideas.

Let's consider the characteristics of flow:

- We become completely involved in an activity.
- Our problems fall away and our inner critic quiets. Nothing else matters.
- We are completing a challenging but doable task.
- Time is distorted as we lose ourselves.
- Being in flow is intrinsically rewarding, and we do the activity because we love it.
- Our creativity, productivity, and wellbeing are amplified.

Another client needed to provide quick answers to the questions of his coworkers, so he kept his door open. While he liked being available to his team, the frequent interruptions weren't helpful when he wanted to focus, and they kept him from regularly enjoying a state of flow. What is your own experience at work?

We need to acknowledge when our offices provide the opposite of flow and become a frenzy of disruptions and distractions. We're jolted from the blissful state and forced to respond to messages, emails, texts, calls, and in-person visits. More than ever, employees need a work environment that promotes a state of flow.

Which of your favorite pastimes help you to experience flow? How can you replicate these experiences? It's important that we spend as much time as we possibly can in this fabulous state.

Tips for Team Leaders

- Consider ways to bring more play into work. You can incorporate contests and challenges to inspire healthy competition. Brainstorming sessions can be wildly creative, and music breaks rejuvenate us.

- Celebrate often! Don't wait until your team reaches its year-end goal; instead, recognize small wins each day.

- Encourage your employees to see setbacks as learning opportunities, every time. Create a safe space so they can openly share with you not only what happened, but how your team might do things differently next time.

- Provide an environment that promotes a state of flow. Give yourself, as well as your employees, permission to tuck away your phones, shut your doors, and respond to messages on a limited basis. When your staff members say they can complete certain projects more efficiently at home, believe them. When you can be flexible about how they meet their needs and complete their assignments, you give them autonomy and build trust within your team.

Whether we're embracing a beginner's mindset or enjoying a state of flow, we are at our best when we're indulging in our creative passions. If you're burning out, these activities can save you. Powerful and potent, they will heal your spirit.

We can do it!

11

BELONGING

I stood in the middle of a crowded room, counting business cards I had just collected during the past hour. Seven . . . eight . . . nine . . . NO. Only nine? I sighed heavily because I still had to talk to another person.

My boss had instructed us to attend this networking event, and to "sharpen our skills," we had to collect the business cards of 10 random people. I'm an introvert, and while I love cultivating meaningful relationships with my major donors, I detest networking events (because of inauthentic small talk and, well . . . *strangers*). I had ample skills and experience to effectively introduce myself and speak well with people, but this didn't mean the exercise was any less draining. All evening, I had watched my extroverted colleagues easily chatting with people, and knew they were in their element.

My mind skipped forward to the dream of recuperating at home, in the company of my dog. I had used up all my inner resources pretending I was enjoying myself, and I didn't dare share my truth with my boss or coworkers. After all, I had been trained since birth that my temperament as an introvert was inherently wrong.

I inhaled and exhaled deeply, as I steeled myself to approach another person. Although I was worn out and craved time alone, I saw a woman standing solo and made my way to her side. While my extroverted colleagues had a blast, I felt like I was being punished that evening as

I slapped a smile on my face and coaxed business cards out of people's pockets. I returned home with 10 cards in my bag, but feeling like I'd abused my soul.

Looking back, I wish that my team had respected our differences at work, and that I could have been my authentic self. Instead, being professional meant that we hid our "undesirable" traits, trying to meet the impossible standards of an ideal employee.

What Is Belonging?

When we belong, we feel valued and respected by our teammates, and we benefit from a foundation of trust that allows us to feel safe being genuine at work. We feel accepted for who we are. In fact, **acceptance** is key to our ability to belong.

To create a community of belonging, successful leaders honor the uniqueness and diversity of their team, rather than perpetuating the myth of an ideal employee.

Our primal need for inclusion runs deep. We're biologically designed for connection and we benefit from being part of a tribe. Imagine an ancestor, eons ago, who had angered the elders and was banished. He no longer had the protection of the group or the safety of the cave, and this exclusion meant certain death, alone in the wilderness.

In fact, our deep-rooted need for belonging is so important that if we don't have it, we may be more likely to flirt with radical ideologies (if the social exclusion occurs along with difficult life events).

If social exclusion paves the path to extremism, then social *inclusion* creates a safe environment to pursue our purpose, discover meaning, and experience profound fulfillment.

In Chapter 2 – Tallying the Costs of Burnout, we discussed the impact of not fulfilling our psychological needs at work. One of those needs is connection, and we thrive in a healthy community. When the environment at work, however, is toxic, we're likely to feel cynical and unhappy that we don't fit in. As we discussed, cynicism is a key symptom of burnout.

Myth of the Ideal Employee

When you agree to work for an employer, you commit to meeting certain obligations. You might successfully work in sprints, where the team pitches in to achieve short-term goals. We need to make sure the overemphasis on work doesn't become a chronic problem, as some managers believe that employees ideally should always be available. Managers who perpetuate the myth of the ideal employee promote unrealistic standards that no one can meet. *No one.*

Here are traits of an ideal employee:

- Is available to work 24/7
- Can complete all work assigned to him, indefinitely
- Is an extrovert who exudes charisma and confidence
- Ensures that her kids don't interfere with work, even if she is a single parent
- Manages to take care of aging parents without impacting her work
- Is a morning person who arrives early and stays motivated
- Can hold her pee all day long
- Believes that a high salary or leadership title equates to long hours in the office
- Has a spouse who helps manage the household
- Can sit all day, without moving his body, while working on the computer
- Finds total fulfillment in his work, and therefore—
- Doesn't desire to explore outside interests and pastimes
- Requires only a few hours of sleep each night
- Is tough and action-oriented (none of this highly sensitive crap)

- Takes her laptop on vacations to show her dedication, and of course—
- Doesn't say NO to protect her boundaries between work and home
- Doesn't burn out, because that's a sign of individual weakness, and certainly not a reflection of systemic dysfunction

Which of these standards of the ideal employee do you still believe? Which ones did you argue about with me in your head? That's a great place to begin exploring.

It's no wonder we suffer from imposter syndrome when we compare ourselves to the ideal employee. We will always fall short, and as we saw in Chapter 8 – Boosting Your Mental Fitness, our internal voices can be vicious. While we crave authenticity, we've trained ourselves to be "professional" at work, which requires that we stifle our basic human needs. Then we muzzle ourselves, for fear our coworkers will know our secret shame—that we are fundamentally inadequate. It's not a surprise that an unhealthy environment that reveres this outdated version of the ideal employee is a sure route to burnout.

What if these fundraisers are successful because of their innate temperament as introverts, not in spite of it? Who better to build meaningful relationships with donors than someone whose brain is wired for deep reflection and authenticity?

Join me in reimagining the ideal employee! Perhaps she's a single mom, juggling work responsibilities with raising her two sons. Perhaps she's an unpaid caregiver, taking care of her dad in addition to working full time. Perhaps he's transgender, wanting to own his body, design his life, and wear different clothes to work. These employees might have physical or mental disabilities. They may celebrate different holidays, speak additional languages, and enjoy diverse customs. We all want and deserve to be included.

You may have come here expecting to learn more about the plight of women in our society (which I'm passionate about, and will discuss at length in a future project). Or you may be expecting me to discuss the nuances of race and belonging. Many great minds are speaking and writing about the need for gender and racial equity, and I support them. Today, however, I'm writing about something different that I dream of for the working world. It's an *equity of temperament*, where we no longer favor extrovert characteristics, but cherish each employee for who they are authentically. (We also no longer favor toughness and grit over sensitivity, and we don't favor morning people over night owls.)

Equity of Temperament

I've heard too many fundraisers who are introverts express surprise for their achievements at work. They say the word "introvert" quietly, as though they're confessing an embarrassing flaw.

This way of thinking perplexes me.

What if these fundraisers are successful *because* of their innate temperament as introverts, not in spite of it? Who better to build meaningful relationships with donors than someone whose brain is wired for deep reflection and authenticity? How much more successful might they be if they stop fighting themselves and honor who they are?

Here's what's really true—the fundraising profession wouldn't survive long without all the traits we bring as introverts. We're key pieces of an important industry. When we feel misunderstood at work, however, it's painful.

I've experienced this myself. I've enjoyed being part of a cohesive and successful team at work, and I've also experienced the opposite—feeling like I don't fit in because I was born to be quiet and thoughtful, rather than gregarious and outgoing. I know well the gut-punch of realizing I'm not part of the team.

The coronavirus highlighted the detrimental ways we already worked, including a bias against introverts. When we don't fit in, it's natural for us to feel cynical about our colleagues, so this is a giant wake-up call! It's time to turn our society upside down and applaud, rather than hide, our remarkable traits of introversion.

Born This Way!

Introverts are introspective, private, and thoughtful, and they recharge by spending time alone. They often think before making decisions and acting. Extroverts, however, are action-oriented and expressive, and they recharge by socializing. There is an introvert-extrovert spectrum that accounts for all our nuances. The brains of extroverts and introverts are different, and we're likely born this way.

As you know, we've admired the traits of extroverts for generations. I had assumed I was in the small minority as an introvert. A recent *Psychology Today* article, however, describes research in 1998 where introverts made up 50.7 percent of the population in a random sample by Myers-Briggs.

Did you get that? *Introverts may make up one-half of the population.* Yet until the pandemic, we lived in a world designed for our outgoing friends. The coronavirus distilled our days into the most meaningful activities, and many introverts thrived with the solitude and focus.

Our rights as introverts, including our need for time alone, have been disregarded. We never again have to consent to believing we are "less than" our extroverted friends.

Celebrating the Spectrum

You can take a quick, online quiz at Introvert, Dear to better understand your own temperament.

Introverts have an opportunity to create a world where we live by our own rules. Let's start by honoring who we really are:

- We do our best work alone, when we can focus intensely.
- We enjoy deeply understanding our relationships as well as our favorite solitary pastimes.
- We prefer in-depth conversations that are meaningful and authentic.
- We enjoy a few close relationships rather than hanging out with a large group.
- We're observant and in tune with our rich, inner world.
- We're expressive writers.
- We're great listeners. In fact, we may listen more than we talk.

In our new world, introverts can decline invitations without giving an excuse or feeling guilty. *Your downtime is sacred*, so don't give it away to please other people who may be judging you for being different.

Extroverts, of course, have their own unique traits:

- They love being with people and feel energized and outgoing when they're socializing.
- They seek novel experiences and new thrills.
- They have fun at parties.
- They are verbally gifted and express themselves well.
- They lose energy when they're alone too much.
- They are known for their friendliness. They're also confident and assertive.

Where on this introvert/extrovert spectrum do you find yourself? We all bring our amazing traits to our jobs, and it's important that we appreciate and respect our differences. We also all fall somewhere along a spectrum of sensitivity.

The Superpowers of Highly Sensitive People

You may not be familiar with people who are highly sensitive, so let me share a bit about myself. When I explain that I can feel both joy and sorrow at the same time, about the same situation, some folks look at me blankly. I cry easily and comfortably, whether I'm gazing at Boo's scrapbook of our favorite memories, or listening to "You Can Go Your Own Way," by Fleetwood Mac. When I see people who are in physical or emotional pain, I feel the empathetic squeezing of my own heart.

It's also true that I often complain about loud sounds, bothersome smells, and uncomfortable fabric. And crowds! I was born this way and have been told throughout my life to *stop being so sensitive*. In high school, I wrote a short story about a powerful girl who willed herself deaf, so the loud noises no longer affected her. She was finally peaceful and happy in the world she created.

As an adult, I discovered that I could concentrate deeply, for hours, and that I'm wildly productive and creative in this state of flow. I play with words as well as photos, and I'm delighted when these activities express my emotional state. I've learned that I love not being interrupted.

At work, I begged the volunteer coordinator to request that a volunteer stop wearing perfume in the office—and while she declined to help me, she rolled her eyes and sighed heavily. *Here we go again; Danielle's being difficult.* I was chided by another colleague for always working in my office with the shades closed. *What's wrong with you? Why are you working in a cave?*

I understand now that I had a right to less stimulation, both at home and in the office. Fortunately, managing my environment has empowered me and helped me create the life I want. Like the heroine in the story who went deaf, I have created a world that soothes me when I feel overwhelmed. My body, mind, and spirit find relief in the sanctuary of my home, as well as in nature.

I'm a highly sensitive person (HSP), as depicted by Dr. Elaine Aron. In her book *The Highly Sensitive Person*, Aron describes people who are in tune with, and sometimes overwhelmed by, their senses and emotions. She estimates they are 15 to 20 percent of the population, and their nervous systems are more aroused than others. She also corrects the misconception that they are fundamentally flawed (this is a personality trait, not a disorder).

In fact, HSPs have exciting superpowers:

- They have a greater awareness of subtleties and details.
- They feel emotions vividly, making them exceptional listeners.
- They process information more deeply and find interconnections.
- They are highly intuitive.
- They enjoy more creativity.
- They can concentrate deeply (ideally with no distractions).
- They serve as sounding boards with friends and offer encouragement.
- They experience deeper bonds and a complex inner life.
- They appreciate beauty, art, and nature.
- They are visionaries, inventors, and artists.

Do you see yourself described here? Or perhaps any of your co-workers? If you're curious about whether you're an HSP, you can take a self-test at hsperson.com (Aron's website) and learn where you fall on the spectrum.

Throughout history, HSPs have used their sensory intelligence about the environment to advise leaders to deliberate before jumping into a rash war. At their best, HSPs stop and think, and then speak their minds to keep the majority from plowing ahead.

People may confuse introverts with HSPs, but they are different. Aron estimates that 30 percent of HSPs are extroverted. The more you can understand yourself, and all your beautiful complexities and nuances, the better. **It's vital that we each know what we need to be at our best.**

In the West, we value toughness, grit, and stoicism, so the ideal in these societies is the opposite of a sensitive person. It's painful to grow up believing there is something wrong with you. Eastern cultures, however, value thoughtfulness and sensitivity, and these individuals likely feel more accepted and appreciated for who they inherently are. No matter our temperament, we all deserve to feel loved and respected.

....

Tips for Team Leaders

- In addition to fundraising, what other professions are successful, thanks to the innate nature of introverts? Consider the positive impact they have on your own industry.

- When possible, allow your employees to choose whether they'll work from home or in the office. Introverts and HSPs discovered the joy of focused, uninterrupted work during the pandemic, and we don't want to go back.

- Remain fair and transparent about how you give promotions and salary increases. It's possible that extroverts and men will choose to work in the office, and they could easily draw attention away from the employees working from home.

- Value the strengths of both introverts and extroverts. Help extroverted team members acquire skills commonly associated with being an introvert, such as listening, writing, and observing. Likewise, constructively help introverts who want to build their skills, such as public speaking (while also recognizing that this will drain their energy, even after they've mastered it.)

- Reconsider the open-plan office. It is challenging for introverts and highly sensitive people to focus and do their best work. If this design must stay, allow employees to use noise-cancelling headphones or to work from home.

- Find out where you fall on the HSP spectrum by taking Aron's self-test at her website. If you are highly sensitive, there's lots to celebrate. Sensitive leaders offer their team compassion, cooperation, and encouragement. They love building consensus and focus on the strengths of their team members. Sensitive leaders are great listeners and are known for letting their staff safely vent without fear of reprisal. Wow! These leaders can be exceptional.

- Don't ask introverts why they're so quiet, implying it's a negative trait. Being quiet means we're processing ideas, and this is normal and good. A fair question is: Why are others so loud?

- Introverts and sensitive people are good listeners, and they want to be heard as well. You can offer them your ear as a leader in a one-on-one meeting.

- Consider the impact that crowded networking events have on your introverted and sensitive employees. How can you set them up for success? They may enjoy the challenge of having a meaningful, transformative conversation with just one person.

No matter your innate temperament, stop fighting how remarkable you are. When you embrace your genuine self, you model for others how good it feels to be authentic, and change can begin in your organization.

We can do it!

12

FULFILLING YOUR PURPOSE

Years ago, before I knew myself better, I accepted a promotion that I didn't really want, but I sure liked the title. And salary.

Never mind that I'd have to manage fundraisers who previously had been my coworkers. Never mind that I'd have less time to do what I most loved in my job (cultivating my donors and writing grants). Never mind that the burden of overwork would drain my energy and dramatically reduce my free time.

I set aside all these niggling, troublesome thoughts, and instead listened to other voices in my head:

You should always accept a promotion, no matter what.
You should go for the highest paying job.
You should be willing to give up your free time, because that's the only path to success.

These voices were loud, and they reminded me of things my family had said or modeled. I let them crowd out the quieter thoughts that would have served me better.

You won't be surprised to learn that, two weeks into my new job as a director, I was miserable. After a development committee meeting one evening, I sat in my newly painted office and cried. I knew I'd made a mistake, and I was already tired from the overtime. I felt frazzled and spent, rather than productive and creative.

I realized I'd listened to outside voices, and not to the grumblings of my own intuition. Although I was distressed, I had clarity that I would never again ignore my own inner compass.

An important step to fulfilling our purpose is identifying our most important values. You and your coworkers will feel immense satisfaction, and perhaps even joy, when you align your choices with your internal guideposts.

Understanding Our Purpose

According to Emiliana Simon-Thomas at the Greater Good Science Center, one of the keys to feeling happy at work is understanding our purpose. When we have a job that reflects our values, and when we understand how our work makes a difference, we're more likely to feel satisfied and fulfilled.

This sounds simple, doesn't it? Yet it's not *easy*. For years, I tried to understand my own choices and behavior. What led me to ignore my internal voice, to my own detriment? How can we feel good at work? How can we help ourselves and our employees experience fulfillment in our careers?

In search of answers, I eventually returned to school to become a professional coach. I wanted to help dedicated leaders who were burning out. While completing my first coach-training program, Dr. Senka Holzer presented her scientific study on her values-coaching technique. Decades of weight lifted from my shoulders!

Senka hypothesized that not only are people unaware they're born with some values, they also don't understand they pick up values along the way. When she began to study people's value systems, she observed we have two completely different sets of values: core and acquired.

Senka shared her biggest ideas in her book *Be You: The Science of Becoming the Self You Were Born to Be.* She delves into why we are unfulfilled in the modern world, based on her values research, and provides science-based solutions.

I had an opportunity to talk with Senka about finding our purpose. We also discuss how our values impact our happiness at work.

Our Values and Our Work— An Interview with Dr. Senka Holzer

Danielle: Understanding our purpose is a huge part of feeling happy at work. Knowing our purpose requires us to understand our values. Why is this so difficult?

Senka: It's challenging because we hold two completely different sets of values. Core values, that we're born with, are our intrinsic guiding principles. I like to say they're part of our "psychological DNA." When our thoughts and actions align with our core values, we're at our best. We feel energized and alive.

> We may be living each day attempting to align ourselves with values that aren't even our own!

Unfortunately, it's challenging to identify our values. And the process becomes even murkier when you consider that we acquire values along the way from outside sources, like our family, social media, culture, and generation. We may be living each day attempting to align ourselves with values that aren't even our own!

Danielle: I've never done that myself [eye roll].

Senka: Sure. Of course you haven't. But if by chance you made decisions in the past—like maybe you accepted a promotion that you didn't really want because you desired the title and the money—then maybe you paid more attention to the outside voices telling you that "appearance" or "status" or "achievement" were more important than your own core values that will ultimately fulfill you.

Danielle: I know now that some of my core values are "creativity," "authenticity," and "adventure." It sure was tough to sort through all the voices and hear myself.

Senka: Exactly. It's tough for all of us. Our core and acquired values greatly affect our thoughts, emotions, and ultimately our decisions. Unless we consciously evaluate and choose which values to respond to, we tend to favor our acquired values.

Danielle: And then we're swimming and sinking in a river of demands. We react to what seems most pressing, or what offers the quickest gratification.

Senka: Here's the rub . . . when we follow the outside voices and pursue our acquired values, we experience only short spikes of satisfaction. Why? Because acquired values don't reflect what innately matters most to us. People who invest heavily in their acquired values (while ignoring their core values) often find themselves hungry for purpose and genuine fulfillment.

Sometimes our acquired values serve us, but sometimes they don't. The key is to understand when we're stuck because outside voices are holding us back.

Danielle: You use a music metaphor, which I find helpful—

Senka: Yes, my clients love this metaphor. When we align ourselves with our core values, it's like playing our favorite music. We feel inspired! Exhilarated! We model for other people how amazing it is to be authentic. We give them permission to play their own music, too.

When we make decisions based on our acquired values, however, it's like playing music, but it's for other people. We may not even like the music, but we play it anyway. Other people don't get to know the "real" us, and so they don't connect in a genuine way.

Danielle: Your scientific study won a first-place research award at a Harvard Medical School conference. Which results were most exciting?

Senka: Our research showed that the more we focus on our core values, the more we'll feel motivated in our jobs. We also enjoy greater wellbeing and satisfaction with life. Our research also showed that this particular coaching technique helps clients to prioritize their core, rather than acquired, values. The positive impact may persist even after the coaching sessions have ended!

The opposite is also true, of course. The more we focus on our acquired values in our daily lives, the less motivated we feel in our jobs. We experience a negative impact on our wellbeing.

Danielle: What happens when our core values match, or don't match, the values of our workplace?

Senka: When our values match the values of our organization, then everything is great. It's possible our values don't match, though.

Danielle: Like if you value independence, and your work environment demands teamwork?

Senka: Exactly. The fit between ourselves and our work isn't perfect, and that's totally normal. If there's a big discrepancy between the two, however, then we need to be careful.

Research shows that people can't remain long in surroundings where our values are greatly conflicting. When the value doesn't fit, change must happen.

We can help the organization to change, but more likely, we'll change ourselves by trying to acquire the values of the organization. Then we're playing music we don't necessarily like, because our environment demands it. Over time, this diminishes our wellbeing.

Danielle: How can this lead to burnout?

Senka: Our gremlins tell us that what we do is never enough, that we need to double our efforts and spend even more hours working. And there is less time in our lives for us to do what makes us happy and fulfilled.

Danielle: Thank you, Senka. I'm so inspired by your work.

I'm certified in Values2Wellbeing, Senka's coaching program that focuses on our core and acquired values. My clients discover the joys of aligning themselves with their core values that they were born with, both at home and at work. They take steps every day toward fulfilling their purpose.

We also explore values they picked up, and we consider whether these values actually serve them. We delve into many of the possible sources of their acquired values, including their country, generation, and family.

Cultural and National Values

My clients explore their experiences abroad and consider political and geographic factors that may influence people's values.

I share with them that I lived in Paraguay for a year, where they valued a laid-back lifestyle. They even had a word for it, "Tranquilopa," a mixture of Spanish and Guarani, which means "Relax already! Everything's fine."

Most families in the village didn't own a car. A car was definitely a luxury.

Compare this to the United States, where we have a go-go-go lifestyle. We value productivity, competitiveness, and independence. Families not only each have a car, but often individuals do. We have multiple cars in every driveway.

What does this mean for our lifestyle? It adds even more intensity. Cars require: the purchase price, gas, a driver's license, state registration, insurance, and maintenance. Not to mention the traffic jams and smog created by our car lifestyle.

Tranquilopa is a Paraguayan value that doesn't fit well in the United States. But I wish it could. What values have you appreciated on your own travels?

Generational Values

My clients love discovering more about their own generation, as well as generations of loved ones.

Each generation forms its own unique values, based on what was going on as we grew up. This is true for Baby Boomers, Generation X, Millennials, and Gen Z, so as we consider our generational values, it's important to remember that, as individuals, sometimes the values resonate with us and sometimes they don't. Whatever is true for you is exactly how it should be. Folks who were born on the cusp between generations have an opportunity as well to decide whether they identify with a particular generation.

When people disparage others by using their generation like it's a bad word, I want to shake the stuffing out of them. "OK, Boomer!" and "Entitled Millennial" might make the speaker feel good in the moment, but it doesn't help us connect to each other or to remember our strengths. In fact, name-calling creates hurt feelings, followed by defensiveness and a spiral to the bottom of bad behavior.

We must remember that we all came of age with different defining moments occurring at home and abroad. In addition, the way our families look changes through the decades, from a nuclear family where mom stays home, to the blended families of today where all adults work. Also, as we come of age, we hear songs for the first time that speak to our souls and make us want to dance, and we fall in love with movies and actors who tell our story.

These coming-of-age differences create different values. Baby Boomers were raised by parents who had endured the Great Depression and World War II. They were taught to work hard, go to college, focus on achievement, and enjoy material wealth.

I happily claim Generation X as my own. We saw the birth of home computers and are ambidextrous in a way that other generations are not, as we're completely comfortable with technology, while also being comfortable with face-to-face personal interactions. My generation values balance, diversity, and freedom and I see these values as key to uniting our country during these divisive times.

Millennials are true digital natives, born with the technology of cell phones, the internet, and email. It's no surprise their social life revolves around the internet. One of the things I most love about the Millennials is their optimistic desire to create change. They're civic-minded and engaged, with big hopes for the future.

Gen Z is already entering the workforce, and it will be fascinating to see what qualities they and future generations will bring, based on their values that were formed as they came of age.

What generational values do you hold? What differences exist between you and your boss? Rather than disparaging each other, let's respect our generational differences. When we approach challenging conversations using the framework of "different values," then it removes the sting of hurt feelings and helps us find common ground.

Inner-Circle Values

Our inner circle includes our close family and friends. Our parents promised us a happy life if we did certain things or behaved in specific ways. Even if what our parents shared made more sense in their own generation, we likely internalized these messages.

As humans, we strive for things we've been taught to value, and we expect the promised happiness after achieving these goals. We might, however, need entirely different things to make us happy.

After we've achieved these goals and haven't found lasting happiness, we often respond in one of two ways: we either try harder and invest even more effort, or we reject the goal and value entirely. What comes to mind as you consider these ideas?

When you catch yourself saying, "I really should . . ." then pay attention. Are you feeling heavy and tense? Are you hunching over from the psychological weight? Is your voice flat and quiet? You're likely encountering an acquired value.

Discovering Your Core Values

You can use this list of clustered values to understand what is most important to you.

Achievement / Accomplishment / Triumph

Adventure / Action / In the moment

Attractiveness / Appearance / Desirability

Awareness / Clarity / Wisdom

Challenge / Competition / Ambition

Cheerfulness / Bliss / Happy spirit

Collaboration / Team / Cooperation

Community / Sharing / Solidarity

Compassion / Empathy / Nonjudgment

Courage / Boldness / Nonconformity

Design / Art / Composition

Devotedness / Dutifulness / Compliance

Discipline / Obedience / Tradition

Ecology / Resources / Preservation

Education / Knowledge / Information

Effectiveness / Focus / Productivity

Endurance / Dedication / Persistence

Intelligence / Brilliance / Talent

Joy / Relaxation / Feeling good

Kindness / Altruism / Humanity

Loyalty / Commitment / Dedication

Money / Wealth / Prestige

Motivation / Guidance / Inspiration

Nature / Environment / Wilderness

Open-mindedness / Tolerance / Flexibility

Optimism / Enthusiasm / Energy

Organization / Structure / Order

Planning / Strategy / Control

Politeness / Manners / Correctness

Purpose / Meaning / Faith

Quality time / Harmony / Pleasure

Respect / Reputation / Influence

Responsibility / Reliability / Accountability

Risk-taking / Excitement / Daring

Experience / Exploration / Variation

Expertise / Mastery / Perfection

Fairness / Equality / Justice

Fame / Popularity / Prominence

Family / Legacy / Heritage

Fulfillment / Peace / Positivity

Fun / Humor / Laughter

Generosity / Hospitality / Philanthropy

Genuineness / Foundation / Consistency

Gratitude / Appreciativeness / Insightfulness

Helping others / Support / Input

Honesty / Trust / Truthfulness

Independence / Self-reliance / Confidence

Self-alignment / Consciousness / Mindfulness

Self-expression / Individuality / Originality

Service / Caring / Charity

Simplicity / Modesty / Humility

Success / Social recognition / Status

Sustainability / Recycling / Conservation

Teaching / Impact / Progress

Understanding / Acceptance / Receptiveness

Vision / Imagination / Ideas

Inner guidance / Inner direction / Intuition

Try on the values and see how they feel, and then select your top 10. After that, whittle your list down to your top three, and notice that this isn't an easy process. It's likely that those three values you identified are your core, and that you'll benefit by aligning your decisions around them.

<hr>

Tips for Team Leaders

- Understand your core values. In addition, understand the impact of the values you adopted along the way. Then choose to align your decisions every day with your core values. Make small changes each day that are sustainable and celebrate your steps forward!

- Pay attention to your values of success, achievement, and perfection. Understand if you acquired them along the way from outside sources. Consider if relentlessly pursuing them will lift you up or grind you down.

- Help your employees understand how their responsibilities transform your organization. Tell them how they're an important part of meeting your mission.

- Learn even more about your employees so you understand what fulfills them, then nurture your staff by assigning them activities that inspire joy at work.

- Reframe a daunting task to reflect your core values. You'll experience greater internal motivation when you understand that your least favorite responsibilities can move you toward your big life goals.

Discovering more about your two sets of values is an exciting journey! Remember that your goal is not to push for big, dramatic change. Instead, you want to make small, daily decisions that are aligned with your core values. Over time, the positive effects will accumulate, and you'll see your life has transformed.

We can do it!

13

CREATING AN INSPIRED LIFE

I had just finished speaking to a ballroom filled with nonprofit employees, relishing what would become my favorite day as a fundraiser. I stood at a lectern above them, and could easily observe their faces, and I was thrilled to see that they were feeling exactly what I had in my own heart—joy and gratitude.

My job at the microphone was to introduce Linda, my creative and trustworthy boss who had guided the organization through a successful capital campaign. As Linda took my place at the lectern, she whispered to me, *"How am I supposed to follow that?"* She had taught me to speak publicly with eloquence and passion, and was surprised I was using these abilities to recognize her leadership.

Months ago, I had nominated her to be honored and was overjoyed when she won. Linda helped me experience a Culture of Wellbeing, before I had the vocabulary or concepts as a coach.

Linda unofficially mentored me, and she helped me understand that successful development directors build relationships not just with the donors, but with the staff and board of directors. It was our job to educate them about the principles of fundraising and demonstrate that the development department can't do it alone. Every person, from the receptionist to the board chair, played a role in taking care of our donors. Linda also taught me the importance of getting the board's support for our annual plan, and when they inevitably brought up the idea of yet another golf tournament, Linda would show them the document and say, *"If we do another event, what other fundraising activities would you like to cut? Or perhaps you'd like to add staff?"* They quickly understood not to mess with the annual plan or the budget. As Linda protected her team from overwork, I felt safe at that organization.

When we launched our multiyear capital campaign, Linda hired a consultant, not with the intention of blaming her if something went wrong, but to follow every bit of her advice. Linda educated the board on what would be required from her team, and she hired additional staff to meet our ambitious goals. Before we began the capital campaign, she advised me to adjust my hours to a 9/80 schedule, allowing me to take every other Friday off. This kept me from feeling overwhelmed during our busiest years.

Linda assembled a dedicated and talented team, and each day, I looked forward to working with its members. Over time, my coworkers became my friends and we shared our personal joys and toughest trials. I remember telling Linda that she was the soul of our team, and she expanded my thinking by saying, *"If I am the soul, Danielle, then you are the heart."*

Wow.

Today, when I think of what a "team" looks like, this is it. I had the privilege of experiencing firsthand this fabulous Culture of Wellbeing, thanks to Linda and my coworkers. When I introduced Linda at the event, I lauded her accomplishments as a gifted leader. I was immersed in gratitude.

Building a Culture of Wellbeing at your organization is an important way to create an inspired life for yourself and your employees. When we enjoy an inspired life, we become the best version of ourselves, and as we self-actualize, each day we choose actions that align with who we are fundamentally. My hope for all of us is that, during our final days, we will experience the fulfillment and deep satisfaction of a life well lived. Creating an inspired life also includes transcendence, where we experience our connection to something greater than ourselves. We intuitively recognize that life is bigger than our own existence, and as we transcend, we connect to the greater good. It's where we say YES to life!

Let's talk about three different ways we can create an inspired life: (1) Experiencing the emotions that help us transcend, (2) Helping others, and (3) Embracing our spirituality and faith.

1. **Experiencing the Emotions That Help Us Transcend**

   Some emotions help us feel less lonely and more connected to others, including gratitude, self-compassion, awe, and intellectual humility.

   Gratitude

   When we feel gratitude, we experience appreciation and thankfulness. While gratitude helps us connect to something larger than ourselves, it also helps people deal with adversity and build strong relationships. Research by Dr. Martin Seligman, the "Father of Positive Psychology," shows gratitude is consistently associated with greater happiness.

   What are you grateful for, at this moment?

   Here are a few ideas for practicing gratitude:

   - Write *a thank-you letter* to someone who impacted your life in a positive way. If you want to spread the happiness, read the letter to that person, and enjoy knowing you're boosting their wellbeing too.

   - Every night, think of *Three Good Things* that you did during the day that you're grateful for. With intention, recall your actions that are leading you to positive change—for example, carving out the time to walk in nature, eating the veggies first on your plate, or calling a friend. Try doing this for seven evenings in a row, and for greatest impact, think of new good things each night.

- Write in a *gratitude journal* each week what you're thankful for.

- When you catch yourself feeling depressed, run through the alphabet, thinking of something you're grateful for from *A to Z*. For example, I'm grateful for: the aurora borealis, bees, chocolate . . .

- If you don't have it in you to be grateful, you can *pray* for the willingness to be more thankful. Likewise, you can *meditate* to clear your mind and open yourself up to positive energy.

- Find a rock or crystal you especially like. Carry this *gratitude rock* with you or set it on your desk as a reminder to take a few moments to feel thankful.

As a coach, I help my clients develop feelings of gratitude. Counting our blessings makes us more resilient and happier.

Self-Compassion

Sometimes my clients share that they need to say unkind things to themselves to be successful. Yet the opposite is true, as we discussed in Chapter 8 – Boosting Your Mental Fitness. When we're compassionate to ourselves, rather than cruel, we can finally be at our best. At last you can soothe yourself, speak kindly to yourself, and know when to ask for help.

Dr. Kristin Neff, a guru of self-compassion, has studied many attributes of this emotion. First, we must be kind to ourselves. We need to recognize the voice of our hateful inner critic and instead choose to treat ourselves the way we'd treat our closest friend. Second, we must remember our connection to humanity. We're not alone in our struggles and everyone else is struggling too, in their own unique way. We can connect to the greater good! And third, we must accept the present moment and experience our emotions with mindfulness. Accepting our internal experience is a key way to reduce our stress. What if, instead of feeling shame that we're overwhelmed at work, we feel self-compassion as we struggle?

Remember that acceptance is not about tolerating bad behavior at work. It's about accepting how you feel on the inside. Imagine how loved you'll feel when you listen to yourself.

What resistance, if any, do you feel when you think about self-compassion? How can you purposefully bring more of it into your life?

Awe

When we experience awe, we're at our best. We move beyond our concerns about our future and worries about our past. You may lose yourself in the present moment, transfixed by the whistle of wind through the branches of the redwood and then the deep call of the raven from atop the canopy. Scenic landscapes quiet your mind and connect you to a higher grandeur.

In addition to experiencing awe in nature, what other activities induce this amazing emotion? Perhaps you feel it when you enjoy your favorite songs, watch your toddler sleep, relish a transcendent meal, or savor works of art. How can you bring more of these awe-inspiring activities into your life?

Pay close attention to how your body feels when you're experiencing awe. Perhaps you feel light and warm, almost effervescent, when you're experiencing awe. Understand what is true for you.

It's not a surprise that research shows that daily doses of awe improve our spiritual wellbeing and provide greater peace of mind. Furthermore, we're more comfortable with solitude when we cultivate awe and connect with the greater world.

Intellectual Humility

We're living in a world where many possess the conviction that their perspectives, attitudes, and beliefs are absolutely correct. These folks see any who disagree with them as mistaken at best, and malevolent at worst. Now, more than ever, we will benefit from intellectual humility, which involves recognizing that our beliefs may actually be limited, perhaps even inaccurate. When we're intellectually humble, we don't feel defensive and are willing to consider other people's ideas and viewpoints.

Research shows that curiosity is a key driver of intellectual humility. People who are intellectually humble are more curious and open to learning. They also are more likely to fact-check false headlines and scrutinize the source, making them less likely to fall for conspiracy theories.

Intellectual humility improves our relationships, as it's associated with empathy and listening to others. We all benefit from acknowledging when we're wrong, and research suggests that followers are more satisfied with leaders who are intellectually humble.

Here are a few tips to cultivate your intellectual humility:

- Before any major conversation or meeting, reflect ahead of time and understand how you ideally want to show up. Then visualize yourself showing up, coming from a place of peace, curiosity, and empathy (rather than a place of ego).

- Understand what success looks like for you in this conversation or meeting, and remember that you don't have control over what other folks say or do. You only have control over how you show up and maintain your presence.

- Before, during, and after your conversation or meeting, come from gratitude, which is the best predictor for intellectual humility. When the conversation doesn't go as planned, use it as a learning experience for yourself and your team.

I believe intellectual humility can play a major role in eradicating burnout. In our society, we believe the destructive myth that burnout impacts the laziest and weakest employees. When we're intellectually humble, we can recognize that our current beliefs are wrong (and that this impacts the most dedicated and passionate workers). We can also see the limitation on our knowledge about wellbeing—and this limitation is what drives me to write this book.

Experiencing the powerful emotions of gratitude, self-compassion, awe, and intellectual humility is one way to transcend and create an inspired life. Another way is to serve our community by helping others.

2. **Helping Others**

Helping people (and animals, plants, oceans, etc.) is the key to us making our way through the dark forest of our fears and finding sunshine again. Not only is it the silver lining to all our setbacks, but it is also a quick route to our own resilience, as it increases our feelings of gratitude and abundance.

Every student in my coach-training class at the local university showed up with scars from life's greatest challenges. It wasn't a surprise when we discovered our niche as coaches was often what we had overcome ourselves personally, from assisting families burdened by cancer to helping employees who were burning out!

If you're thinking, *I don't want to return to school, I want to feel better NOW*, I get it. The interesting thing about helping people is that you can do it in the present, without having made it through the forest. In fact, helping people draws beautiful shafts of sunlight down onto our path as we find our way through.

Science is proving what we intuitively understand. In her book *The Awakened Brain*, Dr. Lisa Miller describes how our brains become healthier when we focus on altruism and love of our fellow humans. Her research suggests that our actionable service may heal our depression. Wow! Furthermore, it's our innate nature to help our neighbors, change our community, and transform our world.

Feeling overwhelmed by your work?

Finish reading this book and choose which dimension you're excited to explore first. You can use the book as a resource when you need it later. Then remember you're not alone, and share this book with your professional community so that others can join you on the journey back to wellbeing.

> It's our innate nature to help our neighbors, change our community, and transform our world.

Feeling disjointed and unhappy from the headlines?

Notice the impact of the headlines on your physical and emotional state, and carve out lots of news-free time in your schedule. Carefully monitor your energy, and at the right time, march in a rally, write your representatives, and volunteer on a campaign. Our democracy needs you now more than ever.

Feeling distraught about the climate crisis?

Learn more about the planetary health diet and consider one small change to your meal planning. In addition, research products that you can incorporate into your lifestyle that are free from plastic and forever chemicals. Gift them to yourself, as well as friends and family. Of course, continue to support your favorite environmental organizations.

Feeling sad and alone?

You can call your own grandma or visit a housebound senior. Looking to make an additional impact? You can volunteer at your favorite nonprofit and help those in need, including seniors, veterans, teachers, children, dogs and cats, etc.

Feeling like something's missing?

You can adopt a dog or cat from a shelter and fill your days with joy. Be sure to read the book *How Stella Learned to Talk*, by Christina Hunger, to give your pet the tools to communicate and find her own sweet voice.

If you want more of something in your life, share it with others and you'll discover it comes back to you in unexpected ways. As you help others, you'll begin to heal, boost your resilience, and enjoy a sense of connection.

3. **Embracing Our Spirituality and Faith**

I'm a highly spiritual person, and I love the idea of being so in tune with the seasons that I shape my life accordingly. For example, spring is a time of rebirth—the perfect time for beginning projects and setting new goals.

Winter, in contrast, is a time of stillness and beauty. In my imagination, there is a hush in the world beyond our cities, as quiet woods are blanketed in snow. Nature holds her breath, anticipating longer days and greener leaves. Winter, at its best, can be a sacred pause for weary souls.

During the holiday season, however, we rush madly in our efforts to maintain traditions and fulfill our "obligations." Our focus is on giving and receiving. We attend parties, gatherings, bonfires, concerts, religious services, and intimate dinners. We forget to breathe.

I remember how the nonprofit world does all of this while attempting to meet year-end goals. Our busyness makes it almost impossible to hear winter's whisper—*this season is not meant to be frantic, but still.* It's a time of reflection, not consumption. It's a time of completion and letting go.

For me, being in touch with nature is a shortcut to the divine. Connecting with nature also means celebrating the winter solstice, the darkest day of the year. At this time, the dark half of the year surrenders to the light. Our ancestors celebrated winter solstice, joyfully welcoming longer days and anticipating the coming of the light. Does nature help you connect to the great, mysterious realm? What shortcuts to the divine can you enjoy?

Some of us practice the faith of a specific religion. Some of us feel a spiritual connection to the universe. Some of us are atheists and agnostics. We must all make room for each other and respect our differences, at work and beyond.

Additional research by Dr. Lisa Miller reveals that when we have intense spiritual experiences, our brains look the same, regardless of whether we're worshipping in a church or reveling in an ancient forest. Furthermore, we all have this part of the brain that we can connect with at any time, whether we're religious, spiritual, or atheist. With each life event, we can choose whether we want to spiral down into worry and isolation or lift ourselves up by engaging in abundance and light.

Knowing that we all use the same spiritual part of the brain, our religious hostilities and wars throughout time become head-scratchers. When we replace the judgment, fear, and dogma with a desire for peace, connection, and understanding, we can remember that we're all in this together, trying to transcend our struggles. Our choices are deeply personal and so are the choices of our neighbors.

Tips for Team Leaders

- We all inherently deserve self-compassion. What is the kindest thing you can say to yourself at this moment? As you boost your self-compassion, it becomes easier to feel compassion for others. How might this transform your team?

- Intellectual humility is a cornerstone of a Culture of Wellbeing. It's possible, however, that you're in a hostile workplace where you don't want to express uncertainty. If this is the case, follow your instincts and turn the hard stuff into stepping stones for your future career.

- What shortcuts to the divine do you personally enjoy? Perhaps prayer or meditation. Think about ways you can access the divine during work hours.

- If you can't be generous with time off in December, encourage your staff to take time in January.

- Celebrate your success in meeting annual goals with all your staff. Celebrate BIG!!!

- Whether or not you meet your goals, be sure you acknowledge the hard work of your staff. Remember that their overtime this past year was time they couldn't spend with their families, or pursuing their own interests.

••

Step by step, we create an inspired life, and what that looks like is unique to each of us. We spend so much time each day at work that it's not helpful to say, "I'll be inspired later, outside of the office." We must create a Culture of Wellbeing, which allows our employees to go home satiated and fulfilled, ready to respond to their own spouses and kids from a place of love and patience, rather than being short-tempered and cross from the exhaustion of burnout.

We can do it!

14

CELEBRATING THAT
WORK COMES THIRD

I'm sitting in my favorite chair, editing chapters I've written for this book. My dog, Scout, has finally settled nearby and curled into a nap. We're together in one of my favorite rooms in the house, with a view of the chickadees, finches, and doves, as well as the squirrels and rabbits. Rather than using bulky sofas and chairs, I designed the room to appreciate the outdoors. There is one simple chair that feels like a rattan throne, and it rests atop of a rug with wild, blue insects. When I sit here, I can see the side patio and all the wildlife.

I finish reading the chapter and set it down, satisfied. Suddenly I wonder, *How many jobs have I had in my entire working career?* I stand and walk to the refrigerator and remove two narrow pieces of paper from the magnetic notepad clinging to the door. Avocadoes dance in shades of green around the border of each sheet. I begin writing, as I track every job, from summer employment in high school to my fundraising career. I noted whether the job helped my wellbeing or diminished it. Then I counted.

I had 16 jobs in my career until I became a coach. Being a coach, author, and speaker is number 17! It turns out that eight of those jobs, 50 percent, weren't good for me. They were draining and stressful, and had

> Understand on a visceral level that you are not the burnout, the stress, the exhaustion, the sniping at your kids . . . this is not your innate nature. We are shining stars!

the same thing in common—my bosses in each of them had leadership issues, from lack of trust to jealousy to micromanaging to taking credit for her team's work.

The other eight jobs were at least decent, if not good, and of those, three were outstanding. What did these three have in common? My bosses in each of them were exceptional. They created healthy cultures where, as employees, we felt safe putting our own needs first. My unscientific poll of my own life reflects the Gallup poll that shows that employees are less engaged and more desperate for better leaders to stop creating and start fixing the external conditions that lead us to burnout.

My Greatest Hopes for You

I want you to understand on a visceral level that you are not the burnout, the stress, the exhaustion, the sniping at your kids . . . this is not your innate nature. We are shining stars! We have an opportunity to celebrate our intrinsic beauty.

I also want you to honor yourself by living your most genuine life. What is more important than our journey of discovering who we fundamentally are? Be bold and be true to yourself, and prioritize your own needs over the expectations of others. Now is not the time to follow the rules and play it safe. At the end of your life, you want to say, *Well done, you.*

As you discover who you are, if you find yourself in a work environment that doesn't value you and makes you feel wrong, it's not a culture that will benefit you in the long run. Remember that you're not stuck and you have options. You might help your current organization to finally allow their employees to prioritize themselves. You might, when you're ready, find a job that already has a Culture of Wellbeing, and enjoy feeling more engaged and appreciated. If you find that you are a valued member of your remarkable team, you can enjoy that sense of belonging and remain at that job as long as you're fulfilled.

Finally, I want you to deprioritize work. You must learn to put yourself first, and then your family, and then your work. You have 10 different dimensions to choose from as you jumpstart your journey back to wellbeing. I believe in you! Also remember that while there are things all of us can do to enjoy greater health, the truth is that if you're burning out, there is systemic dysfunction at your organization, involving leadership issues and unfair conditions.

We have an opportunity to go from individual empowerment to cultural change. A Culture of Wellbeing is the antidote for burnout and our overworked world. Leaders understand that every employee, including the leaders themselves, must put his or her own self-care first. Why? Because we all inherently deserve it, as the shining stars we are. When we prioritize our own needs, we find we can enjoy peak performance at work as well.

Celebrating that *Work Comes Third* is the number one tenet for creating a Culture of Wellbeing. I've developed additional tenets and look forward to sharing those with you in the future!

> We need to empower all employees to choose self-care, without feeling any shame, guilt, or fear of reprisal. When leaders praise the healthy choices of their staff and model wellbeing themselves, then a new culture blooms.

Empowering Your Employees

We have an opportunity to rebuild a world where self-compassion and resilience are fundamental values. We need to empower all employees to choose self-care, without feeling any shame, guilt, or fear of reprisal. When leaders praise the healthy choices of their staff and model wellbeing themselves, then a new culture blooms.

Below are concrete ways we can help employees to choose themselves.

Ethics at Work

Our current understanding of ethics in the workplace is limited, and there has never been a more urgent time to redefine it. Whether you're a fundraiser or a nurse, an attorney or a computer programmer, we need to consider the ethics of self-care. I believe each profession needs a code of ethics that includes our own wellbeing as our number one priority. This frees us up to make responsible decisions to put ourselves first, and this positive choice will reverberate throughout our daily tasks.

Professional Certifications

Professional certifications need to include training to take care of ourselves on all dimensions. The certifying exam should include a thorough understanding of our own wellbeing, in addition to the foundational knowledge of each occupation.

Job Descriptions

Every job description should include the necessity of self-care. While I was a certified fundraising professional for over a decade, today I'm a wellness coach and I agree to conduct that includes "walking the talk" and modelling healthy lifestyle choices. I love this about my job, because it gives me permission to make my own wellbeing a top priority. I wholeheartedly believe other professions will equally benefit.

In addition, include "How Your Role Makes a Difference" in every job description, so employees come on board feeling connected to the mission.

Coaching

To fast-track your organization to a Culture of Wellbeing, hire a qualified coach! Obviously, I am a fan of the coaching profession and the impact we make. I think coaches should be amply trained and then certified by either the International Coaching Federation or the National Board for Health & Wellness Coaching. On your journey back to wellbeing, it's important to choose a talented, certified coach who not only understands your current challenges, but also offers science-based programs to help you love your work (and life) again.

Workplace Book Club

If *Work Comes Third* resonates with you and you're eager for dramatic change in your organization, read this book with your coworkers in your book club. You can talk about one of the 10 Dimensions of Wellbeing each week. At the end of each meeting, encourage participants to share one thing they're taking away and want to apply to their work. Of course, make the book club inclusive and help everyone understand they're invited. If you don't have an official club, you can read the book with your team members and deepen your connection through thoughtful conversations.

Who Do We Want to Become?

We need a Culture of Wellbeing, where employees are cherished, rather than treated as workhorses. We're beyond the tipping point! When we feel accepted for who we are and have a manageable workload, our stress decreases, and our energy and vitality rebound.

What do I personally want to do with this new energy? For me, this means using my creativity and drive to spread the word that *Work Comes Third.*

What about you? What will you do with the extra energy you save from the grip of burnout? Perhaps you're a single parent who wants to have more fun with your kids in the evenings . . . or you're eager to adopt a cat from your local shelter . . . or you're passionate about introducing girls to team sports . . . or you want to sing in your choir, learn to play the guitar, or write your own songs. What will light your fire? Think about the future world you want to create and begin to make it a reality. Who do you want to become? What is your legacy? This is a time to live BIG and in full color. This is a time to live without regrets, creating your best life.

We can do it!

WILL YOU SHARE THE LOVE?

Hey, it's Danielle here.

If you found *Work Comes Third* valuable and know others would consider it to be a game-changer in our working world, then please share this book with your coworkers, colleagues, friends, and family. Special bulk discounts are available if you would like your whole team or organization to benefit from reading this. Just contact me at Danielle@ PrimaveraStrategies.com.

Also, reader reviews are a great barometer of a book's quality. I'm grateful for your online review and rating, wherever you bought the book!

Thank You!

Warmly,

Danielle Collins

BOOK DANIELLE NOW!

Danielle Collins accepts a limited number of speaking and coaching engagements each year. To learn how you can bring her message to your organization, email Danielle@PrimaveraStrategies.com.

ACKNOWLEDGMENTS

I want to thank:

My bosses, who inspired me and showed me that I belong, as well as those supervisors who neglected to do so. I learned from each of them.

My BFF, Celia. Always.

My editorial board (Mary Stallings, Erin Bialecki, and Cathy Fyock) for having the guts to tell me things I didn't want to hear.

Pete, for loving books, seeking answers, and adoring all dogs—even more than I do.

My friends and buddy coaches (Sue, Leslie, Liza, Paul C., and Paul H.) for always listening and, best of all, celebrating.

My high-altitude walking companions, Tiffany and Grace.

My parents, for sharing their love of learning, and my aunt and uncle, for applauding every step to publication.

Senka Holzer, Jim Strohecker, Shirzad Chamine, and Michelle Payne— for creating transformational coaching programs.

My coaching clients, who are utterly inspiring in their sincerity and readiness for change.

The ever-supportive PAGES writing community, offered by Cathy Fyock and Allie Pleiter.

The talented team at Ignite Press, for patiently guiding me through the complexities of publishing.

I want to thank the universe, most of all, for having my back.

NOTES

Chapter 1 – Descending to Burnout

Chapter 2 – Tallying the Costs of Burnout

Many thanks to the World Health Organization World Health Organization. 2019. "Burn-out an 'Occupational Phenomenon': International Classification of Diseases." World Health Organization. 2019. https://www.who.int/news/item/28-05-2019-burn-out-an-occupational-phenomenon-international-classification-of-diseases.

Dr. Richard Ryan and Dr. Edward Deci "Selfdeterminationtheory. org – Page Array – an Approach to Human Motivation & Personality." n.d. https://selfdeterminationtheory.org/.

A position vacancy may create Pepelko, Kristina. 2020. "Untangling Turnover: Why Development Directors Leave and What Nonprofit Organizations Can Do about It." *SPNHA Review* 16 (1). https://scholarworks.gvsu.edu/spnhareview/vol16/iss1/7/.

In a recent Deloitte study "As Workforce Well-Being Dips, Leaders Ask: What Will it Take to Move the Needle?" n.d. Deloitte Insights. https://www2.deloitte.com/us/en/insights/topics/talent/workplace-well-being-research.html.

Chapter 3 – Discovering the 10 Dimensions of Wellbeing

Jim explained that all the dimensions affect the whole Used with permission of Wellness Inventory Certification Training. https://BodyMindSpirit.com (Coach Training).

James Prochaska, PhD, asked Prochaska, James O., and Wayne F. Velicer. 1997. "The Transtheoretical Model of Health Behavior Change." *American Journal of Health Promotion* 12 (1): 38–48. https://doi.org/10.4278/0890-1171-12.1.38.

Discovering the Continuum of Wellbeing Used with permission of John W. Travis, MD, MPH and Wellness Inventory Certification Training. https://BodyMindSpirit.com (Coach Training).

Chapter 4 – Safeguarding Your Sleep

To be at our best CDC. 2024. "Sleep." Sleep. October 18, 2024. http://www.cdc.gov/sleep.

Our bodies suffer as well Gross, Terry. 2017. "Sleep Scientist Warns against Walking through Life 'in an Underslept State' | WAMU." WAMU. WAMU 88.5 - American University Radio. October 19, 2017. https://wamu.org/story/17/10/19/sleep-scientist-warns-against-walking-through-life-in-an-underslept-state/#.Wej6ZZ5fg2M.facebook.

Remove all screens "BWH Press Release - Brigham and Women's Hospital." 2014. Brighamandwomens.org. 2014. https://www.brighamandwomens.org/about-bwh/newsroom/press-releases-detail?id=1962.

The beauty of a power nap Tank, Aytekin. 2023. "The Art of the Power Nap—How to Sleep Your Way to Maximum Productivity." Entrepreneur. August 25, 2023. https://www.entrepreneur.com/living/how-to-power-nap-your-way-to-maximum-productivity/456426.

Chapter 5 – Embracing Nature

The US Environmental Protection Agency KLEPEIS, N., NELSON, W., OTT, W. *et al.* The National Human Activity Pattern Survey (NHAPS): a resource for assessing exposure to environmental pollutants. *J Expo Sci Environ Epidemiol* **11**, 231–252 (2001). https://doi.org/10.1038/sj.jea.7500165.

Our bodies are healthier "PRA - Nature Prescribed." n.d. Parkrxamerica.org. https://parkrxamerica.org/providers/human-benefits-of-nature.php.

add 2.5 years to our lives Kim, Kyeezu, Brian T. Joyce, Drew Nannini, Yinan Zheng, Penny Gordon-Larsen, James M. Shikany, Donald M Lloyd-Jones, et al. 2023. "Inequalities in Urban Greenness and Epigenetic Aging: Different Associations by Race and Neighborhood Socioeconomic Status." *Science Advances* 9 (26). https://doi.org/10.1126/sciadv.adf8140.

spending just 20 to 30 minutes in nature Hunter, Mary Carol R., Brenda W. Gillespie, and Sophie Yu-Pu Chen. 2019. "Urban Nature Experiences Reduce Stress in the Context of Daily Life Based on Salivary Biomarkers." *Frontiers in Psychology* 10 (1). https://doi.org/10.3389/fpsyg.2019.00722.

when we see or hear birds, it boosts our mental fitness Hammoud, Ryan, Stefania Tognin, Lucie Burgess, Nicol Bergou, Michael Smythe,

Johanna Gibbons, Neil Davidson, Alia Afifi, Ioannis Bakolis, and Andrea Mechelli. 2022. "Smartphone-Based Ecological Momentary Assessment Reveals Mental Health Benefits of Birdlife." *Scientific Reports* 12 (1). https://doi.org/10.1038/s41598-022-20207-6.

Unfortunately, almost one-third of adult birds have disappeared Cornell Lab of Ornithology. 2019. "Nearly 3 Billion Birds Gone." Birds, Cornell Lab of Ornithology. 2019. https://www.birds.cornell. edu/home/bring-birds-back/.

are now prescribing visits to nature "Healthy Parks Healthy People: Bay Area." n.d. Healthy Parks Healthy People: Bay Area. https://www. parkrx.org/.

with a higher number of natural killer cells Li, Q., K. Morimoto, A. Nakadai, H. Inagaki, M. Katsumata, T. Shimizu, Y. Hirata, et al. 2007. "Forest Bathing Enhances Human Natural Killer Activity and Expression of Anti-Cancer Proteins." *International Journal of Immunopathology and Pharmacology* 20 (2 Suppl 2): 3–8. https://doi. org/10.1177/03946320070200S202.

Remember that some mindfulness programs "Mindfulness at Work Is Not Mind Control." n.d. Greater Good. https://greatergood. berkeley.edu/article/item/mindfulness_at_work_is_not_mind_control.

Chapter 6 – Nourishing Yourself

Let's talk about the importance of organic USDA. 2024. "USDA Certified Organic: Understanding the Basics | Agricultural Marketing Service." Www.ams.usda.gov. 2024. https://www.ams.usda.gov/ services/organic-certification/organic-basics.

When I learned about the Dirty Dozen Environmental Working Group. 2019. "Dirty Dozen™ Fruits and Vegetables with the Most Pesticides." Environmental Working Group. 2019. https://www.ewg.org/foodnews/dirty-dozen.php.

those who ate right had a lower chance of contracting COVID-19 Halim, Ceria, Miranda Howen, Athirah Amirah Nabilah binti Fitrisubroto, Timotius Pratama, Indah Ramadhani Harahap, Lacman Jaya Ganesh, and Andre Marolop. 2024. "Relevance of Mediterranean Diet as a Nutritional Strategy in Diminishing COVID-19 Risk: A Systematic Review." *PLoS ONE* 19 (8): e0301564–64. https://doi.org/10.1371/journal.pone.0301564.

nearly 60 percent of our daily calories Clapp, Jenifer E., Sarah A. Niederman, Elizabeth Leonard, and Christine J. Curtis. 2018. "Changes in Serving Size, Calories, and Sodium Content in Processed Foods from 2009 to 2015." *Preventing Chronic Disease* 15 (March). https://doi.org/10.5888/pcd15.170265.

eating large amounts of these ultra-processed foods Juul, Filippa, Niyati Parekh, Euridice Martinez-Steele, Carlos Augusto Monteiro, and Virginia W. Chang. 2021. "Ultra-Processed Food Consumption Among US Adults from 2001 to 2018." *The American Journal of Clinical Nutrition* 115 (1): 211–21. https://doi.org/10.1093/ajcn/nqab305.

Even ultra-processed *plant* foods increase the risk Rauber, Fernanda, Maria Laura, Kiara Chang, Inge Huybrechts, Marc J. Gunter, Carlos Augusto Monteiro, Eszter P. Vamos, and Renata Bertazzi Levy. 2024. "Implications of Food Ultra-Processing on Cardiovascular Risk Considering Plant Origin Foods: An Analysis of the UK Biobank Cohort." *The Lancet Regional Health. Europe* 43 (June): 100948–48. https://doi.org/10.1016/j.lanepe.2024.100948.

Research has found that "meal sequencing" Nitta, Ayasa, Saeko Imai, Shizuo Kajiayama, Mikuko Matsuda, Takashi Miyawaki, Shinya Matsumoto, Shintaro Kajiyama, Yoshitaka Hashimoto, Neiko Ozasa, and Michiaki Fukui. 2022. "Impact of Dietitian-Led Nutrition Therapy of Food Order on 5-Year Glycemic Control in Outpatients with Type 2 Diabetes at Primary Care Clinic: Retrospective Cohort Study." *Nutrients* 14 (14): 2865. https://doi.org/10.3390/nu14142865.

Research, however, shows a range of health problems Anderer, Samantha. 2024. "Cannabis Use Linked to Elevated Myocardial Infarction and Stroke Risk." *JAMA* 331 (14): 1172. https://doi.org/10.1001/jama.2024.2075.

Research shows that portrayals of hope "What Makes Positive Content Go Viral?" n.d. Greater Good. https://greatergood.berkeley.edu/article/item/what_makes_positive_content_go_viral.

AI is being developed using the copyrighted works of authors Reisner, Alex. 2023. "Revealed: The Authors Whose Pirated Books Are Powering Generative AI." The Atlantic. August 19, 2023. https://www.theatlantic.com/technology/archive/2023/08/books3-ai-meta-llama-pirated-books/675063/.

we should limit our social media time Hunt, Melissa, Katherine All, Brennan Burns, and Kyler Li. 2021. "Too Much of a Good Thing: Who We Follow, What We Do, and How Much Time We Spend on Social Media Affects Well-Being." *Journal of Social and Clinical Psychology* 40 (1): 46–68. https://doi.org/10.1521/jscp.2021.40.1.46.

research shows phubbing makes people feel unheard Brown, Genavee, Adriana M. Manago, and Joseph E. Trimble. 2016.

"Tempted to Text: College Students' Mobile Phone Use During a Face-to-Face Interaction With a Close Friend." *Emerging Adulthood* 4 (6): 440–43. https://doi.org/10.1177/2167696816630086.

keep your phone out of sight Przybylski, Andrew K., and Netta Weinstein. 2012. "Can You Connect with Me Now? How the Presence of Mobile Communication Technology Influences Face-To-Face Conversation Quality." *Journal of Social and Personal Relationships* 30 (3): 237–46. https://doi.org/10.1177/0265407512453827.

Chapter 7 – Cherishing Your Body

chair-bound for an average of 9.5 hours Matthews, Charles E., Susan A. Carlson, Pedro F. Saint-Maurice, Shreya Patel, Elizabeth Salerno, Erikka Loftfield, Richard P. Troiano, et al. 2021. "Sedentary Behavior in United States Adults." *Medicine & Science in Sports & Exercise* Publish Ahead of Print (July). https://doi.org/10.1249/mss.0000000000002751.

while the average globally is 4.7 hours Mclaughlin, M., A. J. Atkin, L. Starr, A. Hall, L. Wolfenden, R. Sutherland, J. Wiggers, et al. 2020. "Worldwide Surveillance of Self-Reported Sitting Time: A Scoping Review." *International Journal of Behavioral Nutrition and Physical Activity* 17 (1). https://doi.org/10.1186/s12966-020-01008-4.

more likely to develop dementia Raichlen, David A., Daniel H. Aslan, M. Katherine Sayre, Pradyumna K. Bharadwaj, Madeline Ally, Silvio Maltagliati, Mark H. C. Lai, Rand R. Wilcox, Yann C. Klimentidis, and Gene E. Alexander. 2023. "Sedentary Behavior and Incident Dementia Among Older Adults." *JAMA* 330 (10): 934–40. https://doi.org/10.1001/jama.2023.15231.

reduced mortality risk from 8,000 to 10,000 steps Paluch, Amanda E., Shivangi Bajpai, David R. Bassett, Mercedes R. Carnethon, Ulf Ekelund, Kelly R. Evenson, Deborah A. Galuska, et al. 2022. "Daily Steps and All-Cause Mortality: A Meta-Analysis of 15 International Cohorts." *The Lancet Public Health* 7 (3): e219–28. https://doi.org/10.1016/S2468-2667(21)00302-9.

when we absorb them through our skin Oddný Ragnarsdóttir, Mohamed Abou-Elwafa Abdallah, and Stuart Harrad. 2024. "Dermal Bioavailability of Perfluoroalkyl Substances Using in Vitro 3D Human Skin Equivalent Models." *Environment International* 188 (June): 108772–72. https://doi.org/10.1016/j.envint.2024.108772.

Almost all Americans have forever chemicals in their blood CDC. 2024. "Testing for PFAS." Per- and Polyfluoroalkyl Substances (PFAS) and Your Health. November 7, 2024. https://www.atsdr.cdc.gov/pfas/blood-testing/?CDC_AAref_Val=https://www.atsdr.cdc.gov/pfas/health-effects/blood-testing.html.

There are 14,000 known chemicals in food packaging Geueke, Birgit, Lindsey V. Parkinson, Ksenia J. Groh, Christopher D. Kassotis, Maffini, Maricel V., Olwenn V. Martin, Lisa Zimmermann, Martin Scheringer, and Jane Muncke. 2024. "Evidence for Widespread Human Exposure to Food Contact Chemicals." *Journal of Exposure Science & Environmental Epidemiology*, September, 1–12. https://doi.org/10.1038/s41370-024-00718-2.

Chapter 8 – Boosting Your Mental Fitness

Folks with positive mindsets about the COVID-19 vaccine Guevarra, Darwin A., Ethan G. Dutcher, Alia J. Crum, Aric A. Prather, and Elissa S. Epel. 2024. "Examining the Association of Vaccine-Related Mindsets and Post-Vaccination Antibody Response, Side Effects, and Affective Outcomes." *Brain Behavior & Immunity - Health* 40 (July): 100818–18. https://doi.org/10.1016/j.bbih.2024.100818.

we should practice "predemption," Rankin, Kyla, and Kate Sweeny. 2021. "Preparing Silver Linings for a Cloudy Day: The Consequences of Preemptive Benefit Finding." *Personality and Social Psychology Bulletin* 48 (8): 1255–68. https://doi.org/10.1177/01461672211037863.

Chapter 9 – Becoming Your Best at Work

Taking Rejuvenating Breaks Every 90 to 120 Minutes Schwartz, Tony, and Catherine McCarthy. 2007. "Manage Your Energy, Not Your Time." Harvard Business Review. October 2007. https://hbr.org/2007/10/manage-your-energy-not-your-time.

one solution may be *Mandatory Vacations* Pasricha, Neil, and Shashank Nigam. 2017. "What One Company Learned from Forcing Employees to Use Their Vacation Time." Harvard Business Review. August 11, 2017. https://hbr.org/2017/08/what-one-company-learned-from-forcing-employees-to-use-their-vacation-time.

burnout thins the grey matter in our prefrontal cortex Arnsten, Amy F. T., and Tait Shanafelt. 2021. "Physician Distress and Burnout: The Neurobiological Perspective." *Mayo Clinic Proceedings* 96 (3): 763–69. https://doi.org/10.1016/j.mayocp.2020.12.027.

Your behavior impacts how your employees Wigert, Ben. 2020. "Employee Burnout: The Biggest Myth." Gallup.com. March 13,

2020. https://www.gallup.com/workplace/288539/employee-burnout-biggest-myth.aspx.

Chapter 10 – Indulging Your Creative Passions

coined by Mihaly Csikszentmihalyi Oppland, Mike. 2016. "8 Ways to Create Flow according to Mihaly Csikszentmihalyi." PositivePsychology.com. December 16, 2016. https://positivepsychology.com/mihaly-csikszentmihalyi-father-of-flow/.

Chapter 11 – Belonging

describes research in 1998 where introverts made up 50.7 percent "Introvert vs. Extrovert: How Does It Affect Social Anxiety?" 2021. Psychology Today. 2021. https://www.psychologytoday.com/us/blog/sustainable-life-satisfaction/202102/introvert-vs-extrovert-how-does-it-affect-social-anxiety.

She estimates they are 15 to 20 percent of the population The Highly Sensitive Person. 2017. "The Highly Sensitive Person." Hsperson.com. 2017. https://hsperson.com/.

Chapter 12 – Fulfilling Your Purpose

According to Emiliana Simon-Thomas This article originally appeared on *Greater Good,* the online magazine of the Greater Good Science Center at UC Berkeley. Simon-Thomas, Emiliana. 2018. "The Four Keys to Happiness at Work." Greater Good. 2018. https://greatergood.berkeley.edu/article/item/the_four_keys_to_happiness_at_work.

Chapter 13 – Creating an Inspired Life

Research by Dr. Martin Seligman Seligman, Martin E. P., Tracy A. Steen, Nansook Park, and Christopher Peterson. 2005. "Positive Psychology Progress: Empirical Validation of Interventions." *American Psychologist* 60 (5): 410–21. https://doi. org/10.1037/0003-066x.60.5.410.

Dr. Kristin Neff, a guru of self-compassion Neff, Kristin. 2015. "Self-Compassion." Self-Compassion. 2015. https://self-compassion.org/.

we're more comfortable with solitude Yin, Yige, Wenying Yuan, Chenxiao Hao, Yuhui Du, Zhengbo Xu, Joshua A. Hicks, and Tonglin Jiang. 2024. "Awe Fosters Positive Attitudes Toward Solitude." *Nature Mental Health*, April. https://doi.org/10.1038/s44220-024-00244-y.

They also are more likely to fact-check false headlines Bowes, Shauna M., and Arber Tasimi. 2022. "Clarifying the Relations between Intellectual Humility and Pseudoscience Beliefs, Conspiratorial Ideation, and Susceptibility to Fake News." *Journal of Research in Personality* 98 (June): 104220. https://doi.org/10.1016/j. jrp.2022.104220.

followers are more satisfied with leaders who are intellectually humble Krumrei-Mancuso, Elizabeth J., and Wade C. Rowatt. 2021. "Humility in Novice Leaders: Links to Servant Leadership and Followers' Satisfaction with Leadership." *The Journal of Positive Psychology* 18 (1): 1–13. https://doi.org/10.1080/17439760.2 021.1952647.

Chapter 14 – Celebrating That *Work Comes Third*

reflects the Gallup poll that shows that employees are less engaged
Biron, Bethany. 2023. "Employees Are Checked out at Work More
than Ever, and it Doesn't Matter If They're Remote, Hybrid, or Onsite,
Gallup Study Finds." Business Insider. January 25, 2023. https://www.
businessinsider.com/employees-checked-out-work-more-than-ever-
gallup-study-2023-1?op=1.

ABOUT THE AUTHOR

E. Danielle Collins is a former fundraiser and burnout survivor. After going back to school to pursue a career more aligned with her values, Danielle founded Primavera Strategies for Wellbeing. Today, she is a coach dedicated to helping leaders facing burnout to renew their passion. She also writes and speaks about how organizations can cultivate a culture where *Work Comes Third*, empowering them to build thriving teams and fulfill their missions.

Danielle earned her Professional Certified Coach credential from the International Coaching Federation. She is also a National Board Certified Health & Wellness Coach. In addition, in her quest to understand burnout and wellbeing, Danielle is certified in Positive Intelligence®, Values2Wellbeing, and the Wellness Inventory.

Prior to becoming a coach and fundraiser, Danielle earned an MA in Communication Studies from the University of Michigan, and a BA in English from the College of William & Mary in Virginia.

Danielle believes that burnout affects the most dedicated employees, not the weakest. She has lived in seven states and three countries, and currently, she and her dog, Scout, are loving their daily dose of the Rockies.

You can connect with Danielle at PrimaveraStrategies.com.

www.ingramcontent.com/pod-product-compliance
Lightning Source LLC
Chambersburg PA
CBHW071607210326
41597CB00019B/3435